D0554781

Other *For Better or For Worse*® Collections

Retrospectives

Treasury

With Andie Parton

Making Ends Meet

For Better or For Worse® 3rd Treasury
by Lynn Johnston

**Andrews McMeel
Publishing, LLC**

Kansas City • Sydney • London

Andrews McMeel Publishing, LLC
an Andrews McMeel Universal company
1130 Walnut Street, Kansas City, Missouri 64106

www.andrewsmcmeel.com

13 14 15 16 17 SDB 10 9 8 7 6 5 4 3 2 1

ISBN: 978-1-4494-2301-8

Library of Congress Control Number: 2012936733

www.FBorFW.com

ATTENTION: SCHOOLS AND BUSINESSES

Andrews McMeel books are available at quantity discounts with bulk purchase for educational, business, or sales promotional use. For information, please e-mail the Andrews McMeel Publishing Special Sales Department: specialsales@amuniversal.com

Foreword

With two good jobs bringing in a comfortable income, Rod and I did not have the same problems other young couples did. For some of us, making ends meet, even with two parents working, was difficult. The imaginary Pattersons were an average family with typical concerns. During the time in which these next strips were done, I tried to show some of the stress that comes when a mom decides to work outside the home and then discovers that even with a second pay cheque, the family is still living on the edge!

In contrast, I had an amazing job and was able to work from home. My studio was in a paneled downstairs bedroom with ample space for a drafting table and a built-in desk where the kids could sit and draw beside me. I worked every day from nine until noon and again in the evenings after Aaron and Katie went to bed. In between, I was a wife and mother who appreciated all the help I could get!

For Better or For Worse continued to do well in the comics polls. With this affirmation, I had the courage to accept a couple of public speaking engagements (terrifying!!) and go to the Reuben awards, where I met other "new kids on the block" as well as some of my heroes! The Reubens are the Oscars of the comic art industry. Originally, it was an event held in New York by a select group of cartoonists, one of whom was Rube Goldberg, for whom the event is named. He was known worldwide for his crazy mechanical contraptions, which he designed and illustrated. Using numbered instructions, he would lead the reader to follow an egg from the hen, for example, to the frying pan — through a series of impossible maneuvers. My dad was a huge fan, and when I was about eight years old, he took me to a three-dimensional display of Rube Goldberg contraptions at the Art Gallery of Vancouver. I was as impressed as my dad was to see these hilarious drawings come to life. I never imagined that I'd become a member of a society that he'd founded — not knowing that I would become a *Garfield* contemporary and befriend the creator of *Peanuts*, a strip I loved.

Now that I was a member of the National Cartoonists Society, the biggest challenge for me was the writing. If I was going to compete with the talented people already out there and keep my space in the paper, I had to work hard. I also had to draw better and better — which meant showing as much as I could of the houses, their interiors, and the community in which the fictional Pattersons lived. I started to take Polaroid photos of people, places, and things to use as reference. I hired a friend to help me with the colouring of the Sunday pages and to answer the many letters we received. I was determined to reply to everyone who took the time to write. Even if it was a rather standard reply, the signature and doodle were genuine!

In an effort to make the comic strip house less recognizable, I combined the exterior of our Dundas house with the three-floor interior of our house in Lynn Lake — creating an architectural impossibility, but it worked for me! At the same time, our kids were beginning to feel the pressure of being closely connected to the cartoon characters. To protect them from being teased, I kept Michael and Elizabeth in *For Better or For Worse* the same age for three years, allowing Aaron and Katie to grow past them. They then became, in reality, three years older than their cartoon counterparts. This helped a lot.

This treasury includes material from the fall of 1983 to Christmas of 1984. During this time, we moved from Lynn Lake, Manitoba, to North Bay, Ontario. It was a huge change for all of us. The ore in the Lynn Lake mines was quickly running out — people had been warned they would have to make plans to relocate. Many hoped it was just a temporary recession, but it was not. Houses were being abandoned or sold for a song. At this time, you could buy a fully furnished three-bedroom house for as little as $12,000. We sold our lovely home on Eldon Avenue for the price of the remaining mortgage, which was $15,000. We sent our belongings ahead of us and flew our small aircraft to North Bay, Ontario.

My in-laws moved with us. Our new houses were on adjoining properties in the countryside. We chose to live here because we wanted to stay in the north and have some land we could cultivate in an area where there was a diverse, stable economy that would sustain us all well into the future. And it was great to finally have a courier service, which carried my work to Kansas City, Missouri, with door-to-door reliability.

The town of North Bay was soon incorporated into *For Better or For Worse*, becoming a model for fictional "Millborough" — where the Pattersons lived, John had his dental clinic, and Elly worked at the library. Lynn Lake wasn't a place people could readily identify with, and I enjoyed having real material, real structures, and realistic situations to work with. Buildings, businesses, and the kids' schools were all based on North Bay landmarks.

Still, the connection between ourselves and the (now widely) syndicated strip was an obstacle. I tried, in many ways, to separate the fictional stories and characters from the Johnston family. I denied they were us. I said it was all fiction — a figment of my imagination. But, as I reread my work from the beginning, an old adage comes to mind: "Many a truth is said in jest." It's true. I did reveal a great deal of truth. But, after jesting about my family for 30 years, I can definitely say that, "laughter is the best medicine!"

Lynn Johnston

The Arbuckle family lived next door to us on Fifth and Lonsdale in North Vancouver. Their dog, Teddy, was a stoic old guy — trained to follow the footpaths in the garden and to walk alongside his master without a leash. Still, he was always up for a barking session when Alan and I teased him through the fence, which separated our two wartime houses. George Arbuckle worked in the shipyards and was away most days — even on weekends. Mrs A. spent no time with Teddy, and so our teasing was a welcome diversion from pacing the backyard. Teddy barked at us for all he was worth and seemed to enjoy every minute of it. We did not have a tape recorder but managed to bark back at him in such a way that it sounded like several dogs all barking at once. It was a compliment, therefore, to hear from the neighbours on the other side of the street that there had been a pack of dogs behind the Arbuckle house and something should be done about it. Thus, the Ridgway kids made the "news" again.

Dad, Alan, and Teddy the dog.

When a kid is hungry, no explanation for why one should wait will curb the appetite. A kid wants to eat NOW. Dinner time for us was always at 6 o'clock. When Dad came home, nothing was allowed beforehand because it would spoil our appetite. Many a dinner was already "spoiled" because I had to wait so long to eat it!

I don't remember mushrooms being a bone of contention for us growing up because fresh ones were too expensive and canned ones simply disappeared into the stew. Mushroom soup was a staple gravy base and casserole sauce, so it didn't count either. When actual fresh fungi were finally introduced to our palates, we were all grown up. It's our children who have had the luxury of rejecting one of the most delicious culinary delights known to man!

Sometimes, the old chestnut command "If you don't like what we're having, make your own dinner!" backfired. I found the best way to make a less-than-yummy repast disappear was to offer no alternative at all. This, of course, might result in a stoic refusal to compromise followed by a midnight raid on the fridge. The one consolation was that they would eat at midnight the now frigid dinner they'd rejected at 6!

ELIZABETH! — THERE'S NAIL POLISH ALL OVER THE SINK!!

IT WAS A ACCIDENT.

OH, NO! — AND YOU'VE BROKEN MY NEW LIPSTICK!

IT WAS A ACCIDENT.

KIDS! — WHY DID I EVER HAVE KIDS!

DADDY SAYS IT WAS A ACCIDENT.

KNOW WHAT WE NEED, JOHN? WE NEED MORE TIME ALONE TOGETHER.

WE LIVE IN THE SAME HOUSE, EAT AT THE SAME TABLE — BUT WE NEVER SEEM TO REALLY TALK TO EACH OTHER.

AT THIS RATE, WE'LL LOOK AT EACH OTHER ONE DAY — AND WE'LL BE COMPLETE STRANGERS!

WHEN I WAS A KID — I USED TO IMAGINE THE KIND OF MAN I'D MARRY.

I'D IMAGINE HIS FACE, HIS EYES, HIS VOICE, HIS HAIR — EVEN MINUTE DETAILS ABOUT HIS PERSONALITY!

DID YOU DO THAT TOO, JOHN?

SURE.

DID YOUR IMAGINARY GIRL LOOK ANYTHING LIKE ME?

I DON'T KNOW.... I NEVER GOT ABOVE THE NECK.

When I was about 12, I decided to draw the man I would marry. I sat down in my dad's yellow recliner with a pad and pencil and I asked the "spirits" to guide my hand. I drew an average-looking Caucasian man with light-coloured, wavy hair, a nondescript mouth and nose, and large, bright eyes. Once finished, I looked at the face; thinking it was a dumb thing to have drawn, I wadded up the paper and threw it away. Wow. I don't know how many times I wished that I had kept that drawing!!!

Having a syndicated comic strip into which I could pour my frustration saved my sanity. In fact, this was a common occurrence with my kids — this simple situation was enough to drive a parent crazy. I got a huge amount of satisfaction from drawing screaming kids with their mouths wide open and tears flying from their eyes. Exaggeration is the key to making art come to life; to be able to turn life into art was a godsend … and that's no exaggeration!

This strip was done for Loretta Clarke, who was one of my dearest Lynn Lake friends — and continues to be so. The two of us worked together on boards, events, and charities. We could always count on the other to show up, work hard, and clean up when the party was over. Talented, intelligent, honest, and fair, she is one of my favourite people in the world. Having said that — we were always so busy that we rarely took the time to really sit down and enjoy each other's company (I had my family and the strip; she had four daughters of her own and a career). One day, in the Hudson's Bay store, we ran into each other. It was a rare opportunity. We had a few moments to spare and tried to have a conversation around the demands of my son, who kept interrupting. I did this strip as a sort of apology and to let her know that I care for her and truly enjoy her company!

A couple of years ago, we took a three-week trip to Mexico together. We never tired of each other's company for a minute — it took all that time just to catch up!

Loretta and me in Mexico.

I swore I wouldn't raise my children in front of a television. I said daytime t.v. was a bad influence and a waste of time. Then I bore children — and I blessed the channels that brought us the likes of *Mr. Rogers*, *Polka Dot Door*, and *Sesame Street*. I knew when these shows were coming on, I memorized their theme songs, and I encouraged my offspring to partake. I learned that the media sometimes does have a message: Moms, take a break when you can and don't feel guilty about it!

I used cloth diapers for my first child and was proud of myself for doing so. I breastfed, made my own baby food, and sterilized everything. I followed guidelines and kept a diary of how much Aaron ate, when he slept, and for how long. I was going to be the perfect mom! Then when Katie was born, I relaxed — I did what felt right and was safe and made sense. I learned that there's no such thing as the perfect mom, or the perfect kid — you just have to do what works for both of you.

I loved making up names. When I thought up the word *Grubberware*, it immediately conjured up the idea of a party where toilet brushes, rubber gloves, plungers, and other unattractive bathroom cleaning stuff would be displayed and sold. This meant I could draw toilet-related stuff (which was rather discouraged) and possibly get away with it. I guess there's a part of me that will always want to bug the guy in charge.

KLUMP
CLOMP!
KLUMP
KLACK
CLACK!
CLUMP
KLAK
"CLUMP

LOOK, DADDY! — I GOT MOMMY'S DRESS ON — AN' HER MAKE-UP AN' HER SHOES!

CAN I GO OUT ON HALLOWE'EN LIKE THIS?

WHY NOT?

— IF IT'S GOOD ENOUGH FOR YOUR MOTHER.....

Thanks to my mother-in-law, Ruth, we have always had a costume box. Anything remotely useful was squirreled away into a trunk in the basement — whatever was in there could be sacrificed to the gods of creative expression. When it was too cold to play outside, when Halloween was nigh, or when boredom set in, this box came to the rescue. When we moved, even though we had too much stuff, we had to bring it with us — some things are too much fun to throw away!

Our refrigerator was our timetable, gallery, and photo wall. On it were hand-painted cards, personal reminders, pictures, and grocery lists — a good slam would cause an avalanche of paperwork to hit the floor. It was like an historical cache of information, documenting everything from first report cards to notes from the tooth fairy. This humble appliance was as important on the outside as it was within!

I rarely encouraged a sales party at my home, but when you're in a small town, you have to participate or you won't get invited to the next one! The husbands usually planned a guys' night out at the same time — somewhere away from the party, but within crawling distance from home!

A couple of years ago, I did this same thing. But instead of coming home with a pile of pumpkins, I came home with bushels of apples and peppers — I just couldn't resist!

My mom had a big yellow mixing bowl, which was used for just about everything. She was an excellent baker — when she made cookies, the dough was as good as the hot-out-of-the-oven cookies themselves. It wasn't enough for me to have the spoon, the mixer blades, and the spatula — I had to try and lick the bowl as well!

After reading *Tom Sawyer*, I was convinced that spooks really did come out at night. My dad was no help; he loved to tell ghost stories. The Brothers Grimm book was a favourite of my grandfather's. Between the two of them, my brother and I were reluctant to go out in the dark until the year that my grandma gave us flashlights for Christmas. We used these to expel ghosts from corners, creeps from closets, and bugs from the bed sheets, until the batteries ran out!

Like my mother, I couldn't resist the hungry faces of kids at the door. It's amazing, isn't it, how fresh baking makes folks magically appear.

Home sales parties always involved a lot of work for the hostess. Because we were all too familiar with the local bakery, homemade goodies were a must: squares, cookies, fruit-filled tarts, finger sandwiches, and other dainties — the ladies who made the best turnouts got the best turnouts! When it was my turn to host, I was in a panic. Not having my mom's cooking skills, I couldn't hope to compete. Still, ladies came to my house … perhaps out of curiosity, perhaps out of compassion!

Our front door led directly to the back door, which meant we had a "shotgun hallway" — if somebody put a shot through the front door, it would exit out the back. This created a perfect flue. When both doors were open, the draft sucked everything down the hall and into the rooms on either side. This was an efficiency of filth if there ever was one. I began to vacuum on calm, rainy days only.

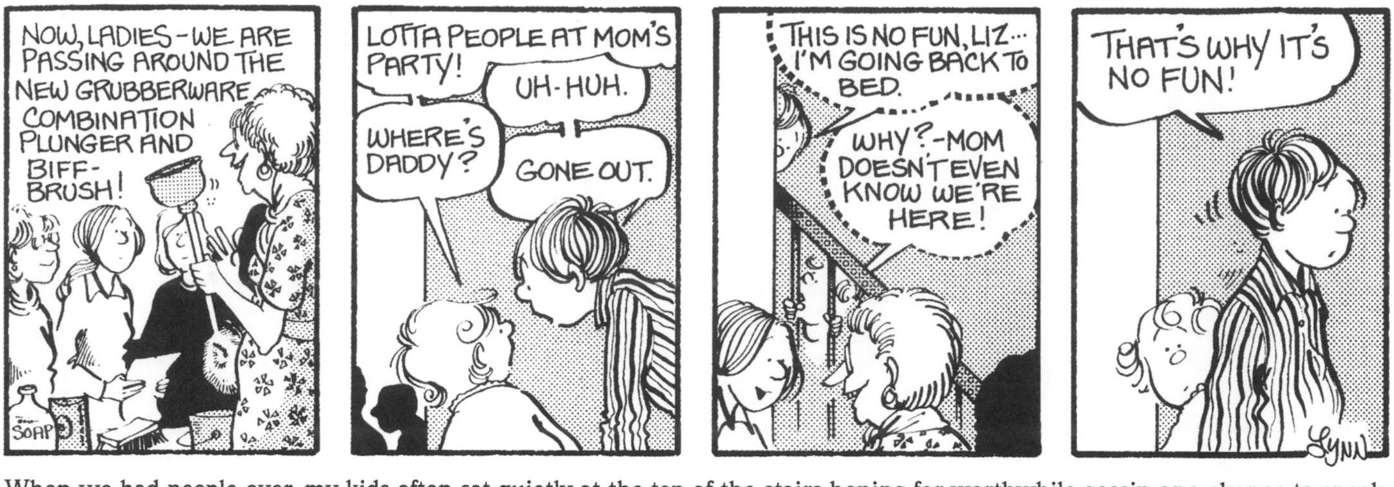
NOW, LADIES - WE ARE PASSING AROUND THE NEW GRUBBERWARE COMBINATION PLUNGER AND BIFF-BRUSH!
SOAP
LOTTA PEOPLE AT MOM'S PARTY!
UH-HUH.
WHERE'S DADDY?
GONE OUT.
THIS IS NO FUN, LIZ... I'M GOING BACK TO BED.
WHY?-MOM DOESN'T EVEN KNOW WE'RE HERE!
THAT'S WHY IT'S NO FUN!
LYNN

When we had people over, my kids often sat quietly at the top of the stairs hoping for worthwhile gossip or a chance to sneak into the kitchen and swipe some goodies. I knew they were there. I could easily have shoved them off to bed, but as long as it wasn't a school night, I figured, out of sight, out of mind. This liberty came to an end when Aaron, after a huge ingestion of pop, decided to burp the alphabet. The hallway created the perfect amplifier. He was in bed by the time he got to "P."

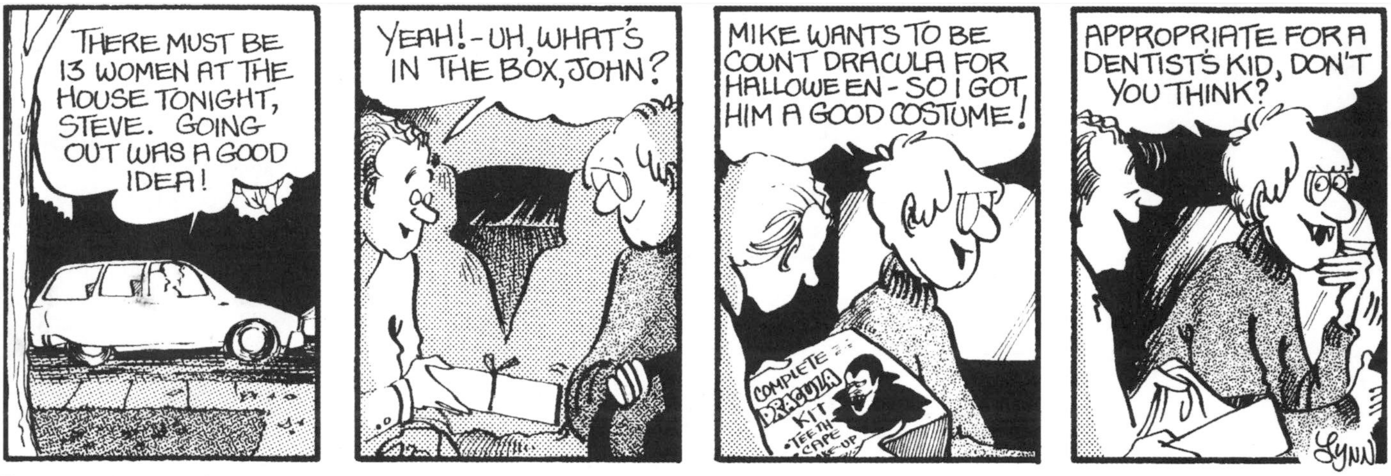
THERE MUST BE 13 WOMEN AT THE HOUSE TONIGHT, STEVE. GOING OUT WAS A GOOD IDEA!
YEAH! - UH, WHAT'S IN THE BOX, JOHN?
MIKE WANTS TO BE COUNT DRACULA FOR HALLOWEEN - SO I GOT HIM A GOOD COSTUME!
COMPLETE DRACULA KIT
APPROPRIATE FOR A DENTIST'S KID, DON'T YOU THINK?
LYNN

Because this storyline took place in late October, I had to make up something that would cover both the houseware party and Halloween. Imagining that John had picked up a costume for Michael created an opportunity to have some fun.

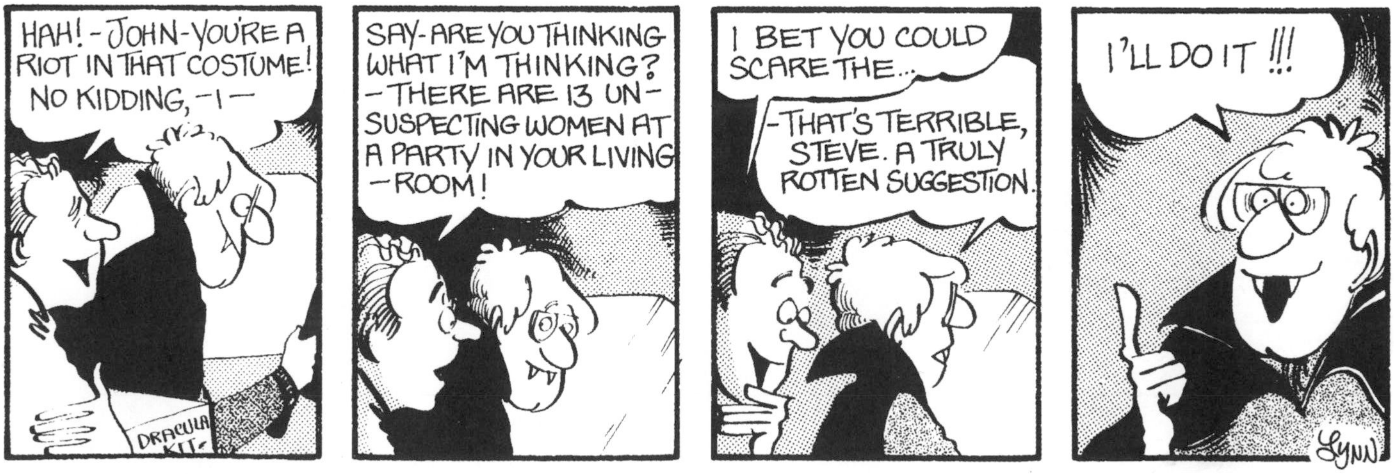
HAH! - JOHN - YOU'RE A RIOT IN THAT COSTUME! NO KIDDING, - I -
DRACULA KIT
SAY - ARE YOU THINKING WHAT I'M THINKING? - THERE ARE 13 UN-SUSPECTING WOMEN AT A PARTY IN YOUR LIVING - ROOM!
I BET YOU COULD SCARE THE...
- THAT'S TERRIBLE, STEVE. A TRULY ROTTEN SUGGESTION.
I'LL DO IT !!!
LYNN

This isn't something my husband would have done, but I would!

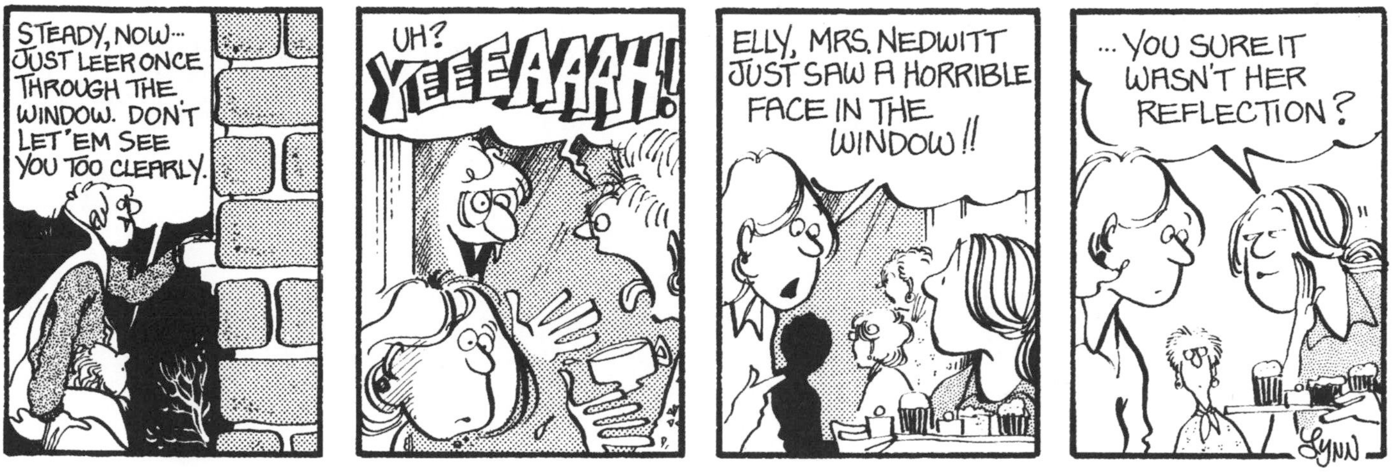
STEADY, NOW... JUST LEER ONCE THROUGH THE WINDOW. DON'T LET'EM SEE YOU TOO CLEARLY.
UH? YEEEAAAH!
ELLY, MRS. NEDWITT JUST SAW A HORRIBLE FACE IN THE WINDOW!!
...YOU SURE IT WASN'T HER REFLECTION?
LYNN

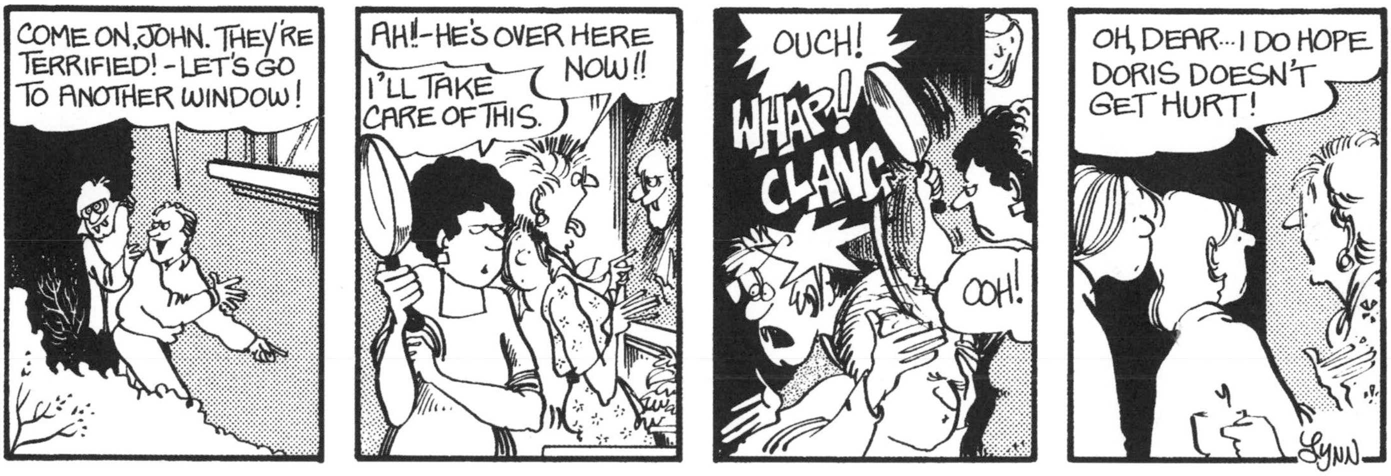
COME ON, JOHN. THEY'RE TERRIFIED! - LET'S GO TO ANOTHER WINDOW!
AH!!-HE'S OVER HERE NOW!!
I'LL TAKE CARE OF THIS.
OUCH!
WHAP!
CLANG
OOH!
OH, DEAR... I DO HOPE DORIS DOESN'T GET HURT!
LYNN

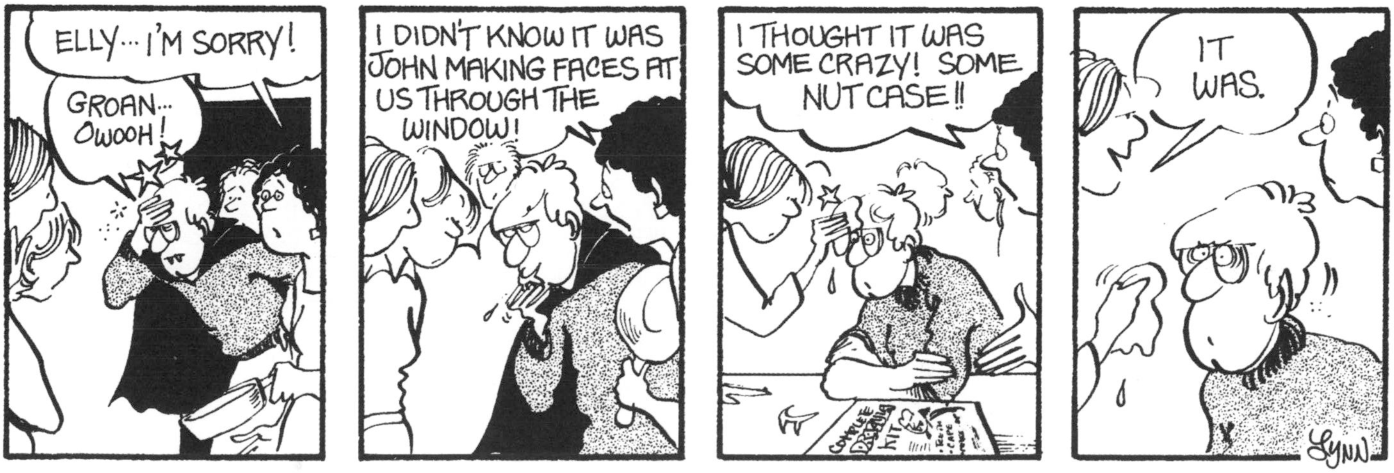
ELLY... I'M SORRY!
GROAN... OWOOH!
I DIDN'T KNOW IT WAS JOHN MAKING FACES AT US THROUGH THE WINDOW!
I THOUGHT IT WAS SOME CRAZY! SOME NUT CASE!!
IT WAS.
LYNN

One year Rod made me a set of false teeth that went over my real ones. They were so realistic that you couldn't tell they were fake. After the kids were done with their door-to-door trek on October 31, the adults would carry out a Lynn Lake tradition called "trick-or-drinking." When costumed revellers would show up at your door, you had to invite them in for a drink — and if you couldn't guess who they were, you'd have to wait until the following morning to find out!

The night I went trick-or-drinking, I wore a white-blonde wig, a Dolly Parton–style outfit, and my false teeth. In a British accent I'd learned from my mother, I greeted our wary hosts, who repeatedly begged me to tell them who I was. I was one of the few revellers that night who got to do the big reveal the following day.

The problem was also compounded by the fact that the kids never liked those odd-coloured, molasses tasting, wax paper wrapped toffees that you only see during the last days of October — they'd always leave them for me. These ugly things are still given out at Halloween, they still taste the same, and I still like them!

16

Like so many, I would rather buy a can of pumpkin filling or purchase a whole darned ready-made pie than go to the trouble of making one myself. In reality, I have only once cooked and eaten a pumpkin. In this one true-to-life case, I did cook our Halloween pumpkin and learned a valuable lesson: Never cook a pumpkin you've used as a Jack-o-lantern ... it tastes like *#$%!!!

There were times that I did outshine my mom-in-law, but it was not in the pie-making department. I made great casseroles, soups, and stews; she did the breads, the roasts, and the baking. Both of us were fine in the veg department, so between Ruth and myself, we provided our men-folk with some mighty fine grub. There's nothing like two women in the kitchen — especially when they're both a bit competitive!

The changing of the seasons has always been a reminder that time goes by more quickly than we realize and that nothing stays the same. It was my parents-in-law who often reminded us to appreciate each other.

The original Farley really did love chewing gum. I discovered his penchant for gum when I saw him take some out of a wastebasket, work the Kleenex off it, and continue to chew for some time without swallowing. I had never seen a dog do this before, so Farley's gum chewing became a bit of a party trick. He particularly liked Juicy Fruit — even if it had been previously enjoyed. The thing was to make sure I was there when he spat it out, or I'd have a surprise on my foot later on.

Katie getting into the Halloween candy.

Here is another true-to-Johnston-life happening. Rod decided to carry on his father's tradition of making pancakes on Sunday morning but cancelled his next performance due to lack of interest. In colder climates, even pancakes aren't enough to make one leave a warm, toasty bed!

My mother-in-law, having been an elementary school teacher for many years, readily took on the challenge of teaching our children whatever they hadn't been able to grasp in school. She once used a fresh pie to help Aaron learn fractions. My dad-in-law was in the room when she asked, "What do we call the biggest piece of pie?" and it wasn't Aaron who answered but Tom who, smiling easily, said, "Mine!"

Aaron was recently reminiscing about the great lunches I used to make for him: "Other kids might have a slice of cheese and some dry, white bread — but we got a great big, honking SANDWICH!" Katie didn't share his enthusiasm: "I used to trade mine with a boy who always had sugar sandwiches." (She's always had a sweet tooth.) I wasn't angry that Katie had given her lunches away — considering the poor diets of some kids, he probably needed a good, nutritious lunch more than she did.

When I did this drawing, I actually felt my arm waving in the air desperately wanting to answer a question — it brought me back to my grade school days. I never missed an opportunity to show off. It was always disappointing to have the teacher ask someone else, someone less energetic than myself. There is one serious drawback to being chosen after such a wild display of shoulder-wrenching arm gestures, however: If you get the answer wrong, you look pretty darned silly!!

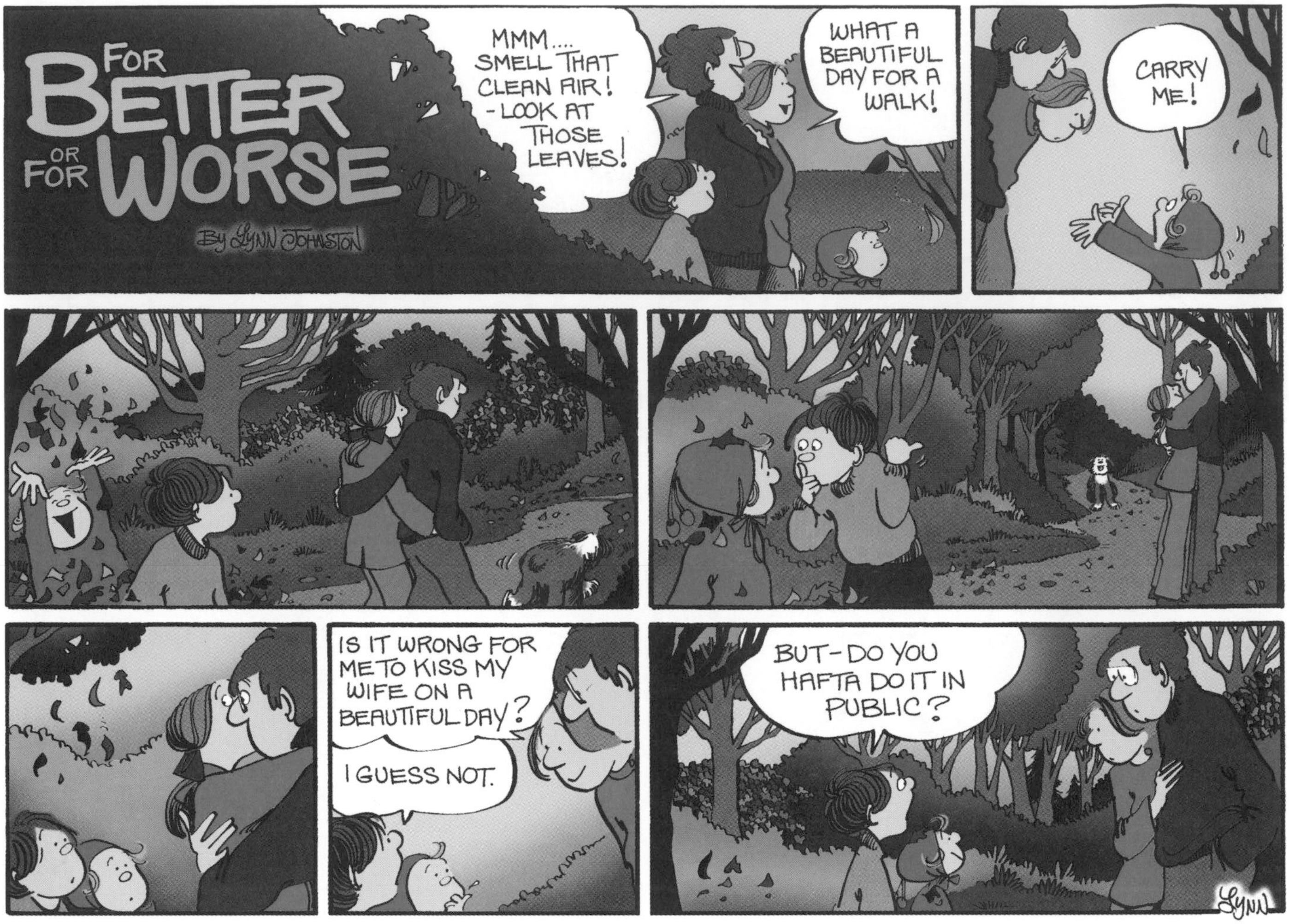
FOR BETTER OR FOR WORSE
By LYNN JOHNSTON
MMM.... SMELL THAT CLEAN AIR! - LOOK AT THOSE LEAVES!
WHAT A BEAUTIFUL DAY FOR A WALK!
CARRY ME!
IS IT WRONG FOR ME TO KISS MY WIFE ON A BEAUTIFUL DAY?
I GUESS NOT.
BUT - DO YOU HAFTA DO IT IN PUBLIC?
LYNN

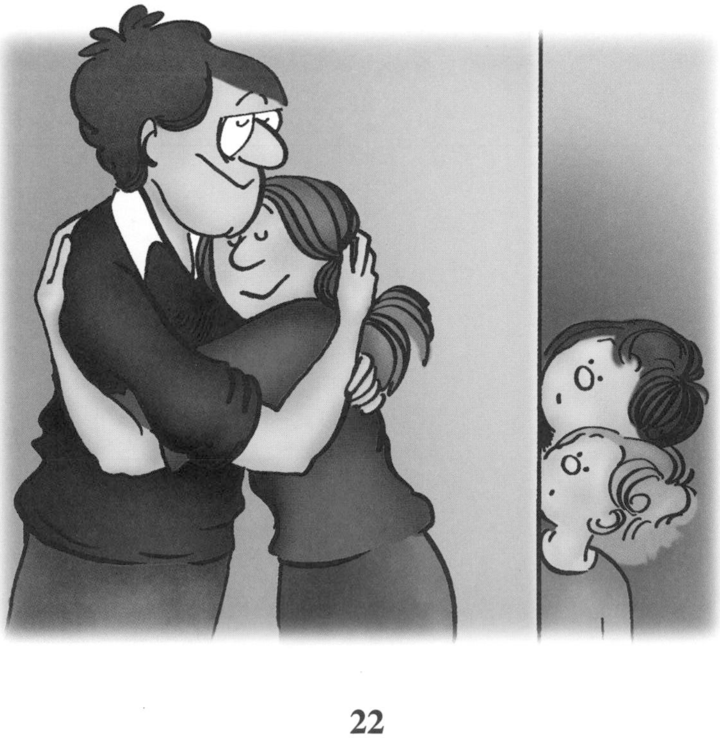

Aaron and Katie were both independent children. Trusting and eager to explore, they enjoyed Kindergarten, Saturday art classes, junior skating, and other activities that required them to be separated from Mom and Dad for a period of time. I credit this not just to parenting but to the wonderful daycare workers, playschool teachers, babysitters, and other caregivers who worked with them during their formative years. Together, we instilled confidence in themselves and confidence in us. We were really fortunate to have such a responsible, trustworthy team of people to back us up and give the kids a healthy, enjoyable, and safe environment to grow up in.

There always has to be a villain in the classroom, someone who bullies and "breaks the law" — that's just the way it is. I bet we can all remember the names and faces of the kids who made our own young lives miserable.

I had two nemeses in elementary school — I can still picture them. I can remember the fear I had lying awake at night knowing that I would have to face them. I was a bit of a bully in my own right; I could fight tooth and nail if I had to, and I'd win. I wouldn't prey on just any kid, I'd go after the mean ones — the ones I thought deserved a good pummelling!

24

Brad, for me, embodied a number of kids I knew as a child, who were ready to hit and to hurt for no reason at all.

I loved comic books and considered myself a superhero. Not a female superhero with a huge bust, skimpy costume, and impossible sexy powers (these women were Barbies compared to me!) — I was a REAL superhero. If I saw a smaller kid being bullied by a bigger kid, I'd take the guy on — even if it meant getting my dress torn or my face bloodied. I was a fighter, and when the mood struck, the energy I could put into a good punch-up amazed me.

I remember breaking a girl's finger once, because she wouldn't let go of my hair. The more she twisted my hair, the harder I bent her finger. Afterwards, I sported a bald patch and she wore a cast. Our parents forced us to make up. They couldn't believe the ferocity of our battle. We were both angry kids. It took a long time before either of us realized that we weren't angry with each other — we both were unhappy with our homelife and didn't know how to deal with our emotions.

25

My taste in comics was much more tame than Michael's. I loved *Little Lulu*. She was a real girl with ordinary looks, cool friends, and a great imagination. I also loved the Disney books — Donald and the kids and Scrooge McDuck topped the list. I wondered what Scrooge did with a house-sized bin full of money. If it was mine, I'd have given it all away. I never imagined that I'd get to know two of the Disney writers who wrote those very books ... but that's another story!

My mother suggested I try and get to know the kids I was fighting with, to try and understand them, see where they lived, find some common ground. In a couple of instances, this worked. Carol, the girl whose finger I broke, became a friend of sorts. We continued to have our differences, but with few kids our age in the neighbourhood, we eventually got along. Another truce was made with a boy called Murray, whose mother was a widow and was raising four kids. I felt sorry for him.

I continued to fight and make up and fight all through elementary school. It was just the way things were. I was too young to see the whole picture, and I'd often wind up looking at negatives.

This positive little episode resulted in many letters — mostly from teachers and social workers who used these panels to illustrate things they had been trying to talk about: bullying, tolerance, and compassion. No parable here was unintended. By talking about ordinary things that happen to ordinary people, I'd often open a floodgate. So many things that should be resolved … aren't. It was surprising to find that my work was being seen as an opening for discussion.

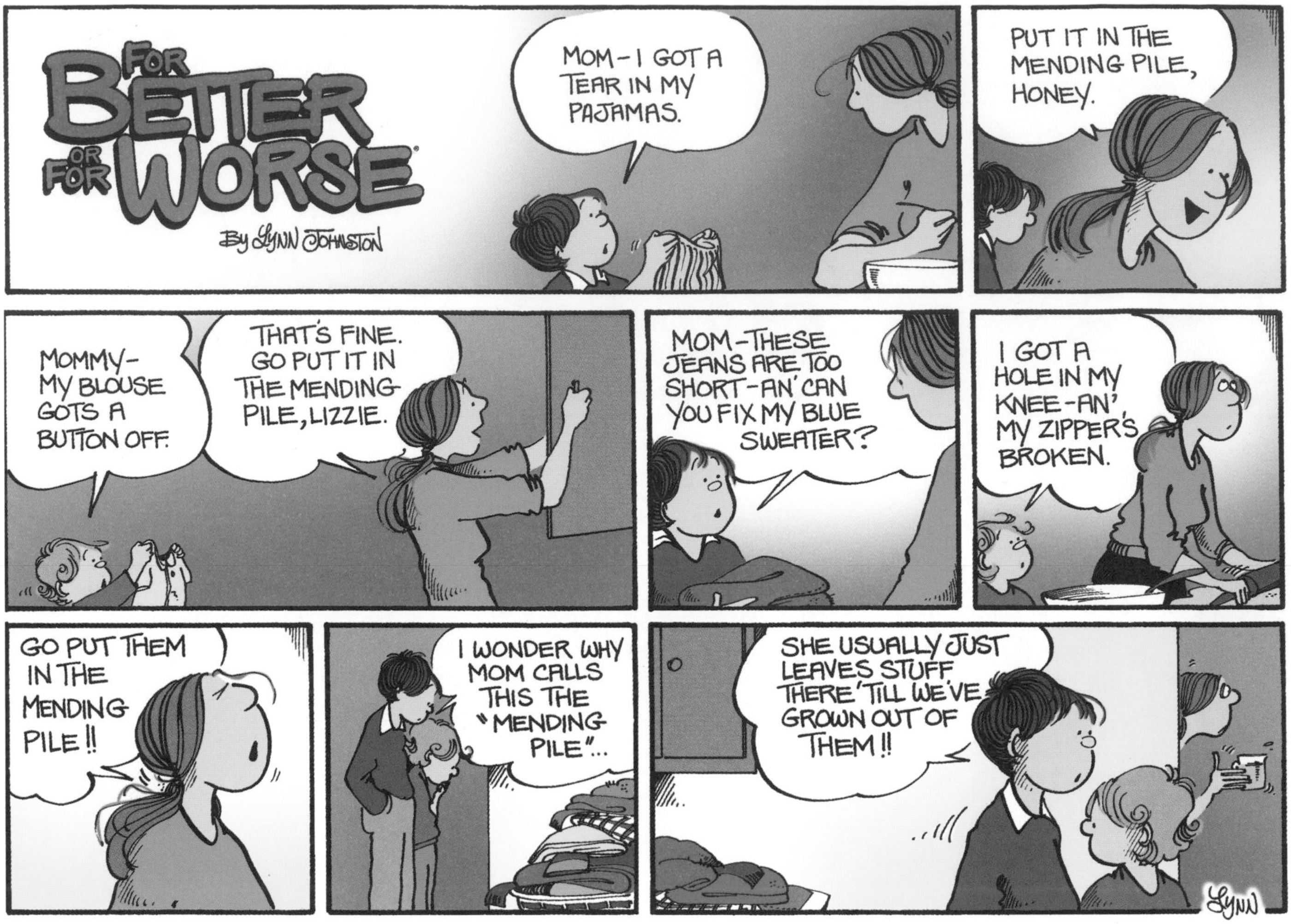

FOR BETTER OR FOR WORSE
BY LYNN JOHNSTON
MOM - I GOT A TEAR IN MY PAJAMAS.
PUT IT IN THE MENDING PILE, HONEY.
MOMMY- MY BLOUSE GOTS A BUTTON OFF.
THAT'S FINE. GO PUT IT IN THE MENDING PILE, LIZZIE.
MOM-THESE JEANS ARE TOO SHORT-AN' CAN YOU FIX MY BLUE SWEATER?
I GOT A HOLE IN MY KNEE-AN' MY ZIPPER'S BROKEN.
GO PUT THEM IN THE MENDING PILE !!
I WONDER WHY MOM CALLS THIS THE "MENDING PILE"...
SHE USUALLY JUST LEAVES STUFF THERE 'TILL WE'VE GROWN OUT OF THEM !!
LYNN

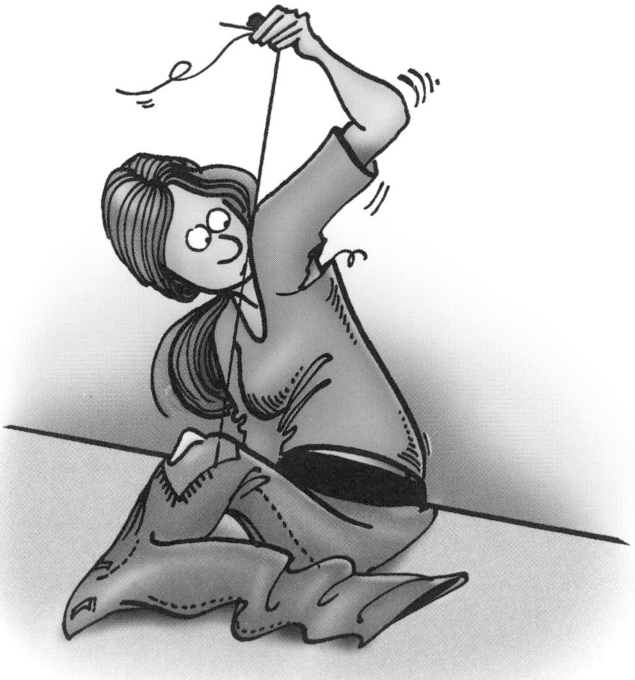

This little snowsuit, Katie actually wore. It was one of my favourites and when I washed it, I foolishly put it in a hot dryer. It came out looking like a scraggly, matted sheep, and I cried when I saw it. Kate didn't seem to notice and happily wore it until it became too small. At the time, my mother's creed was, "If it doesn't go into the washer and dryer, it goes OUT!" After this, I became much more practical. I bought things that could be easily laundered, and I made sure I was aware of her favourite things. My motto was, "If it's cute and she likes it — LOOK AFTER IT!"

Once again, I grit my teeth and told a tale that actually happened.

We were in a dark, high-end restaurant in Winnipeg.

June Willis was not an actual name. These people were fictional.

With arrogance and purpose I walked up to the couple I had been staring at ... to discover they were complete strangers. By telling such tales on myself, I was hoping to both cleanse my soul and warn others to MYOB!

Comic-strip artist Lynn Johnston resists the idea of moving to the United States. 'I'm a real Canuck,' she says.

Portable artist leaving Manitoba

By Paula Martin

The woman whose cartoons are syndicated in more than 500 newspapers world-wide left the interview to go in search of a new sewing machine.

Lynn Johnston, whose comic strip, For Better Or For Worse, reaches readers in 10 countries, is in Winnipeg on the first leg of a promotion of a new compilation of her work, It Must Be Nice to Be Little, and a National Film Board documentary, See You In The Funny Papers, in which she is featured.

Johnston, also known to Manitobans as a Lynn Lake resident, will soon be leaving the province to take up residence in North Bay, Ont., where the family has purchased some land. Johnston says she is "portable," but adds she feels almost apologetic about leaving.

"On the other hand, it's time for us to go," she says.

With Lynn Lake's uncertain future-because of possible mine closings, Johnston says the town has become unstable and is shrinking rather than growing, adding "the more and more depressed the community became, the more and more attractive this (North Bay) property started to look."

And, her work demands that she travel a certain amount. With the airlines cutting back on some northern flights, getting about can become difficult, she says.

But the family won't move from their home of six years until Katie, five and Aaron, 10, finish school in the spring, she adds.

Although her agent has hinted that perhaps she might move to the United States, Johnston is having none of it.

"I'm a real Canuck. I had no idea that I was so nationalistic," she says.

Johnston also expresses strong feelings about bilingualism. Her children are learning French and she says that one day she would like to learn the language herself. She adds that she is looking forward to living in northern Ontario because of the small French community nearby.

Not learning a second language is "like closing doors," Johnston says, adding that some day she would like to move to an area that is strongly bilingual.

After an afternoon of back-to-back interviews, she comments that she'll try not to be "boring," explaining that people often believe cartoonists ought to be as witty as their creations sometimes are.

Johnston has even changed her hairstyle so she doesn't look like the cartoon's Elly Patterson, a character she says people sometime expect her to resemble.

The situations and dialogue contained in For Better Or For Worse are contrived, Johnston explains.

"You don't have conversations like that," in real life, she muses. "If you sat and looked in on a normal family, you would soon fall asleep."

"You talk to people who don't exist and you have adventures with people who don't exist," when devising the dialogue and characters for the cartoon.

Although Johnston protests the comparison, she concedes that some of the characters' behavior may resemble that of her family especially the "prattle between husband and wife."

She describes her dentist husband Rod as the more entertaining of the two, the one who can spout one-liner jokes at random.

As her own family grows up, it might be more difficult in the future to chronicle the day-to-day growth of little Lizzie and Michael in the comic strip. Although their situations are not really duplications of what her own two children experience, she says readers often assume so.

"Even today the kids sort of cringe when they think of what's being printed."

Katie, she says in not that interested in the comic strip, but Aaron is "one of my harshest critics" who reads and re-reads the cartoons and has to hoard her book collections because she tends to give them away to visitors at her home.

This photo of Lynn Lake was taken from the headframe of the local mine, coincidentally named Farley!

This is the front of our home on Eldon Avenue. It was a nice house, the interior of which was mirrored (approximately) in the strip. This house, our cottage on Berge Lake, plus wonderful family and friends made living in this remote area easier!

We didn't have a chainsaw — we didn't need a chainsaw ... but for some reason known only to men, my husband bought a big one, with all the safety gear that went with it!

This is another personally experienced scenario, which reached the papers. Even though we admonished the combatants, we laughed all the way to the food court!

My dad took us to the Hudson's Bay store one year to see Santa. We were a bit too old to do the Santa thing, but this was something we felt we were doing for Dad. He was in a great mood and enthusiastically encouraged us to wait in a long line. As we stood there, he went on and on about the decorations and the scene in which Santa had been placed. I remember thinking that he was way more excited about this than we were. Eventually, Alan and I had our turns on Santa's lap, were photographed, given a candy cane, and allowed to go. Dad was beaming, and on the bus heading home, he quizzed us about our Santa experience. "Well," I said, "he was greasy and smelled like cigarettes and needed to use a toothbrush really badly."

Alan added, "His beard wasn't real and didn't fit right, and I didn't like the way he said 'Ho, Ho, Ho'." Dad looked out the window of the bus for a while and said little else about the our trip to see the great Claus. When we got home, I overheard Dad talking to Mom about our excursion. As it turned out … the man who was dressed as Santa was a great pal of our dad's!

I have always wondered what it is that makes boys and men want to run around shooting each other, when a really good, moderated argument would resolve almost anything. My thinking is: If women ruled the world, we'd get the politics over with expediently, thereby saving the civilian population, then do our best to rejuvenate each other's economies by shopping! This said by someone who admits to having been a street fighter at the age of five!

The one time I remember going Christmas shopping with my dad was the time he decided we needed a new couch for the living room and wanted to buy one for Mom for Christmas. Bad idea. We bought a squared-off, ugly beige thing with fabric that felt like the rough side of Velcro. Mom hated it … but, true to form, she never complained. They had that awful couch until they moved out of the house on Fifth Street. The next couch they had, she bought — with no input from Dad. Fair is fair!

38

This comes from a joke my dad used to tell about a man and his son who got onto an elevator. I can't recall the joke, but I always remembered the punch line, which was: "If anyone hears anything or smells anything — it's my dad!"

This story was a made-up scenario. A sort of feel-good Christmas story, which eventually became the outline for an animated special called *The Christmas Angel*.

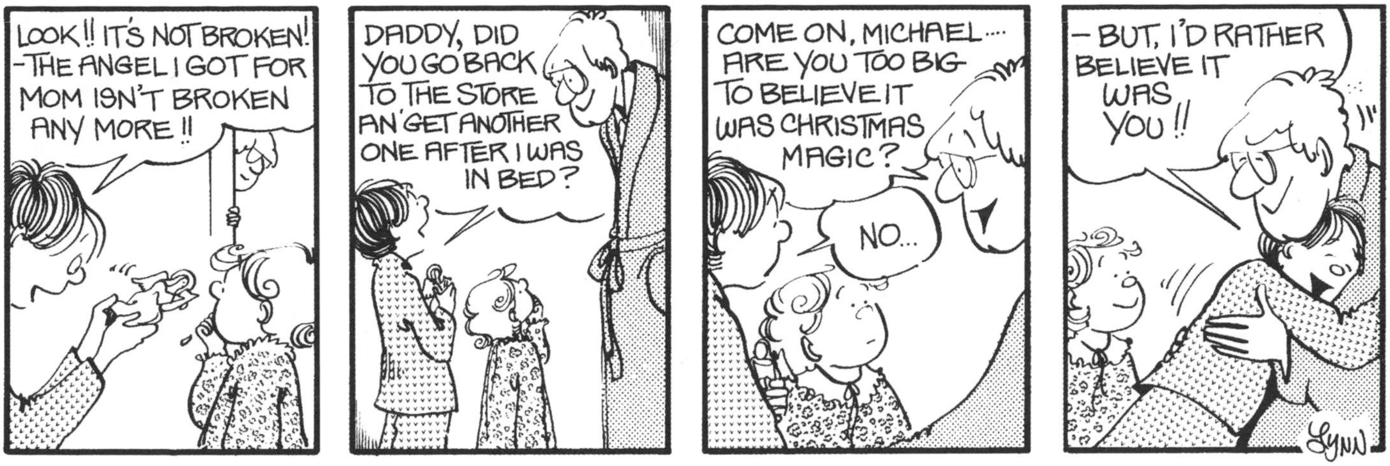
LOOK!! IT'S NOT BROKEN! -THE ANGEL I GOT FOR MOM ISN'T BROKEN ANY MORE!!
DADDY, DID YOU GO BACK TO THE STORE AN' GET ANOTHER ONE AFTER I WAS IN BED?
COME ON, MICHAEL.... ARE YOU TOO BIG TO BELIEVE IT WAS CHRISTMAS MAGIC?
NO...
- BUT, I'D RATHER BELIEVE IT WAS YOU!!
LYNN

This was the kind of magic my dad would have performed; he was just like that.

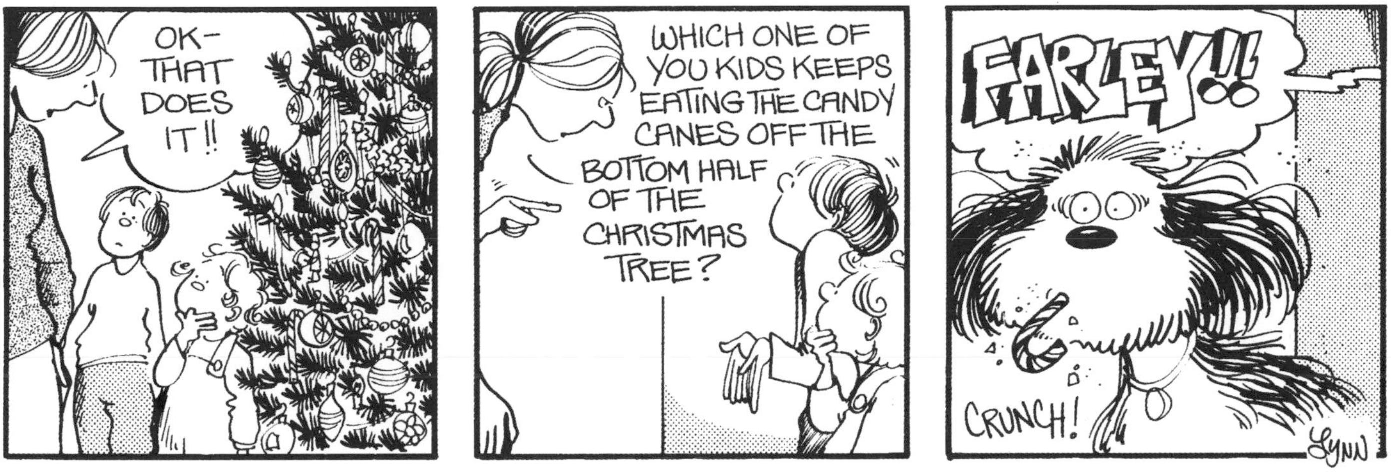
OK- THAT DOES IT!!
WHICH ONE OF YOU KIDS KEEPS EATING THE CANDY CANES OFF THE BOTTOM HALF OF THE CHRISTMAS TREE?
FARLEY!!
CRUNCH!
LYNN

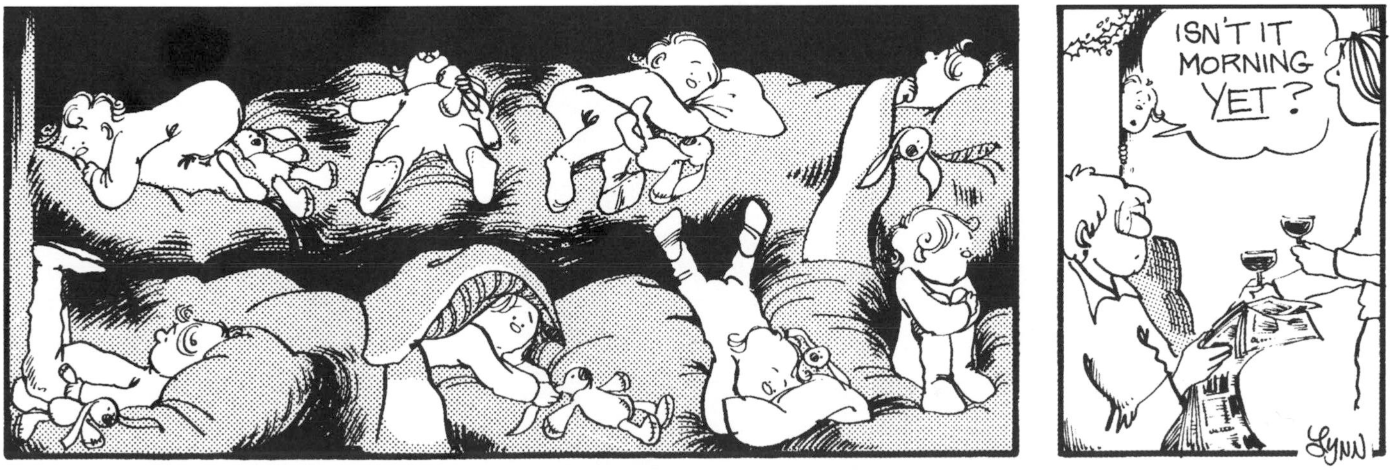
ISN'T IT MORNING YET?
LYNN

My bed had a white headboard and, for as long as I can remember, a violet, flowered bedspread. I would turn it into a vehicle, a flying carpet, or a tent in the wilderness — and with each incarnation came a different position for sleeping. I used the pillow for everything from a headrest and chest protector to a dashboard and helmet. The blankets could be a cloak, a tent, or a capsule in outer space. In my bed, my imagination went wild, which was good thing … because I was sent to my room a lot!

Once in a while, I would put a bit of religion into Christmas and Easter strips to prove that I DID know the reason for the celebration and to assuage the readers who thought I was far too focused on the commercial aspects. I could guarantee three kinds of mail when a strip like this was released: One came from the Christian right, who asked that much more focus be put on ecclesiastical issues; one from the atheists, who felt that I was pushing religion down their throats; and finally the moderates, who appreciated the occasional reminder that festivals like this deserve a nod to the deity for whom the chocolate was fashioned and the bells were tolled. Again, I tried to answer every letter I received. Even if I disagreed with someone's philosophy, I certainly appreciated the time they took to write to me.

This is one of the strips I actually used in an effort to find someone. The names "Stan, Gretchen, Barb, and Kenny" appeared on a Christmas card with no last name and no return address. I never did find out who they were ... so if you're reading this, folks, and you sent a card to the Johnstons in 1983 ... this is why you never got one in return!

After this strip appeared, the quote "Mom's having another one of her fat days" became part of our collective vocabulary.

44

One of Rod's dentist friends actually did wire a woman's teeth together after she demanded he do so in order to help her lose weight. With the wiring job, he gave her a set of wire cutters so she could open her mouth immediately in case of an emergency. I think she lasted about a week before she cut herself loose!

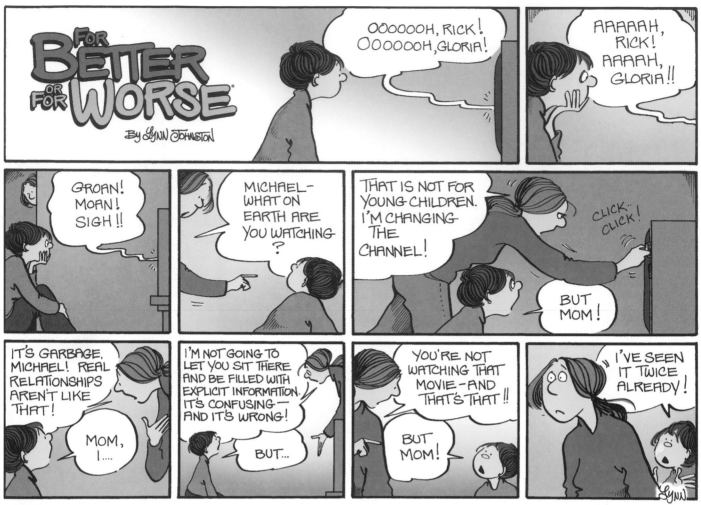

I recently watched a series on HBO that showed not only the most graphic violence but some of the most explicit sexual scenes I have ever witnessed! Naturally, I wouldn't want young children to see stuff like this. I thought it was over the top and unfit to show as family entertainment. I watched the entire series, glued to the set, and was sorry when it was over.

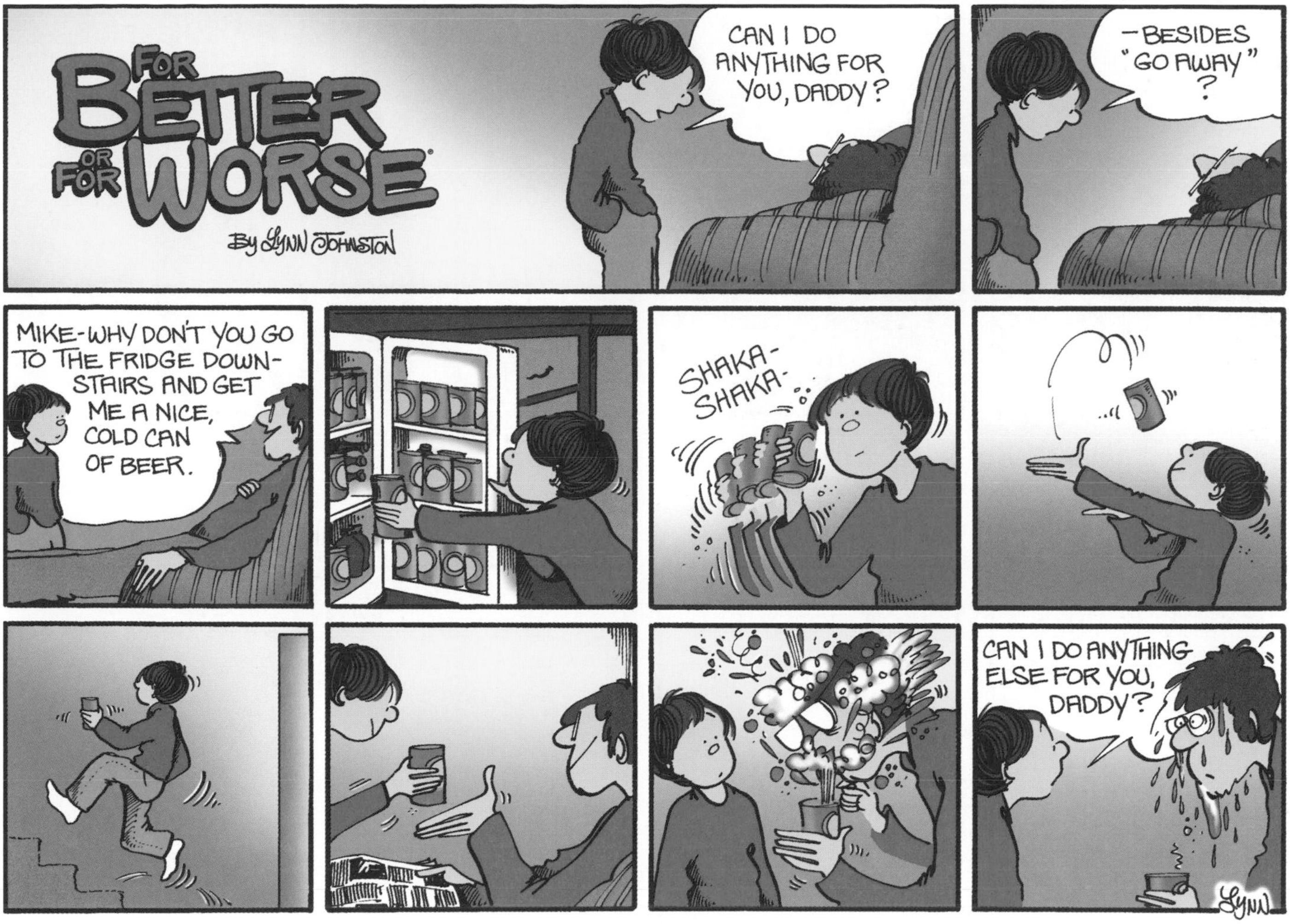
FOR BETTER OR FOR WORSE
BY LYNN JOHNSTON
CAN I DO ANYTHING FOR YOU, DADDY?
—BESIDES "GO AWAY"?
MIKE-WHY DON'T YOU GO TO THE FRIDGE DOWN-STAIRS AND GET ME A NICE, COLD CAN OF BEER.
SHAKA-SHAKA-
CAN I DO ANYTHING ELSE FOR YOU, DADDY?
LYNN

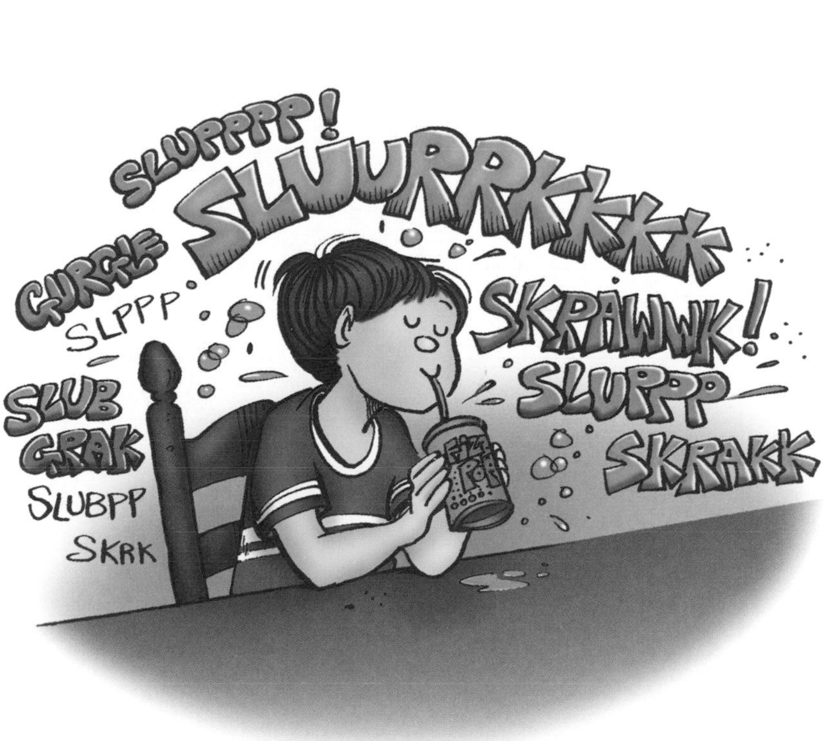
SLUPPPPP!
GURGLE
SLUURRKKKK
SLPPP
SKRAWWK!
SLUB
SLUPPP
GRAK
SKRAKK
SLUBPP
SKRK

These cartoons were done after we moved from Lynn Lake to North Bay, Ontario. After being part of a regularly scheduled exercise group in a space I could walk to, I was now 20 minutes away from a gym and had no friends to work out with. In an effort to guilt myself into exercising again, I drew these and published them, knowing full well I was doing nothing at all!

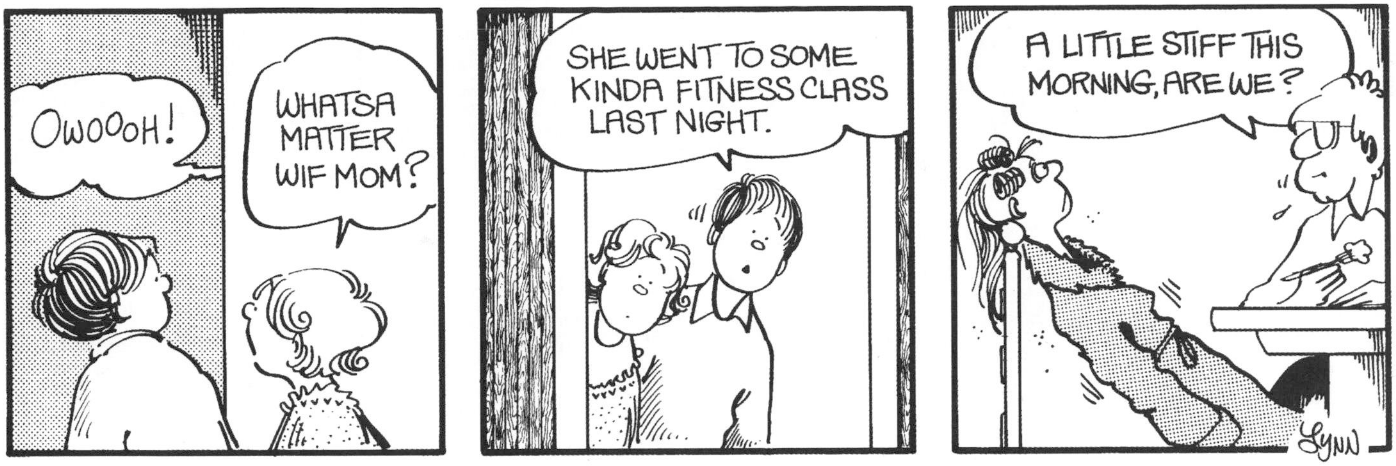
OWOOOH!
WHATSA MATTER WIF MOM?
SHE WENT TO SOME KINDA FITNESS CLASS LAST NIGHT.
A LITTLE STIFF THIS MORNING, ARE WE?
LYNN

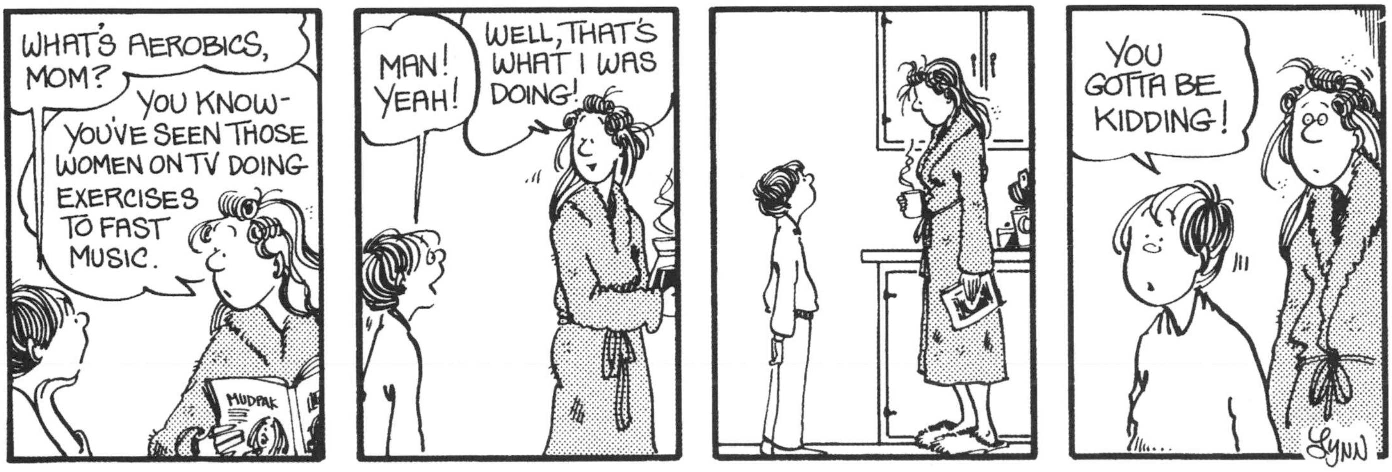
WHAT'S AEROBICS, MOM?
YOU KNOW- YOU'VE SEEN THOSE WOMEN ON TV DOING EXERCISES TO FAST MUSIC.
MUDPAK
MAN! YEAH!
WELL, THAT'S WHAT I WAS DOING!
YOU GOTTA BE KIDDING!
LYNN

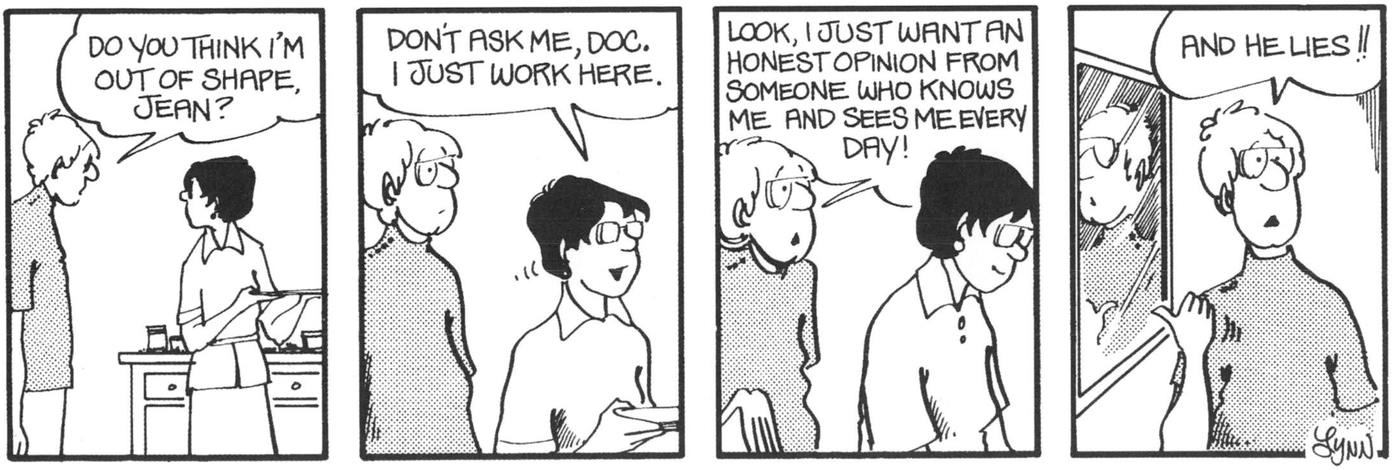
DO YOU THINK I'M OUT OF SHAPE, JEAN?
DON'T ASK ME, DOC. I JUST WORK HERE.
LOOK, I JUST WANT AN HONEST OPINION FROM SOMEONE WHO KNOWS ME AND SEES ME EVERY DAY!
AND HE LIES!!
LYNN

Here, chauvinist Ted tries to influence John Patterson to be a bit more assertive when it comes to women. As far as I know, my husband had nobody like this in his circle of chums, but it was necessary to insert a character who was not exactly likeable or practical — to help create and support new dialogue.

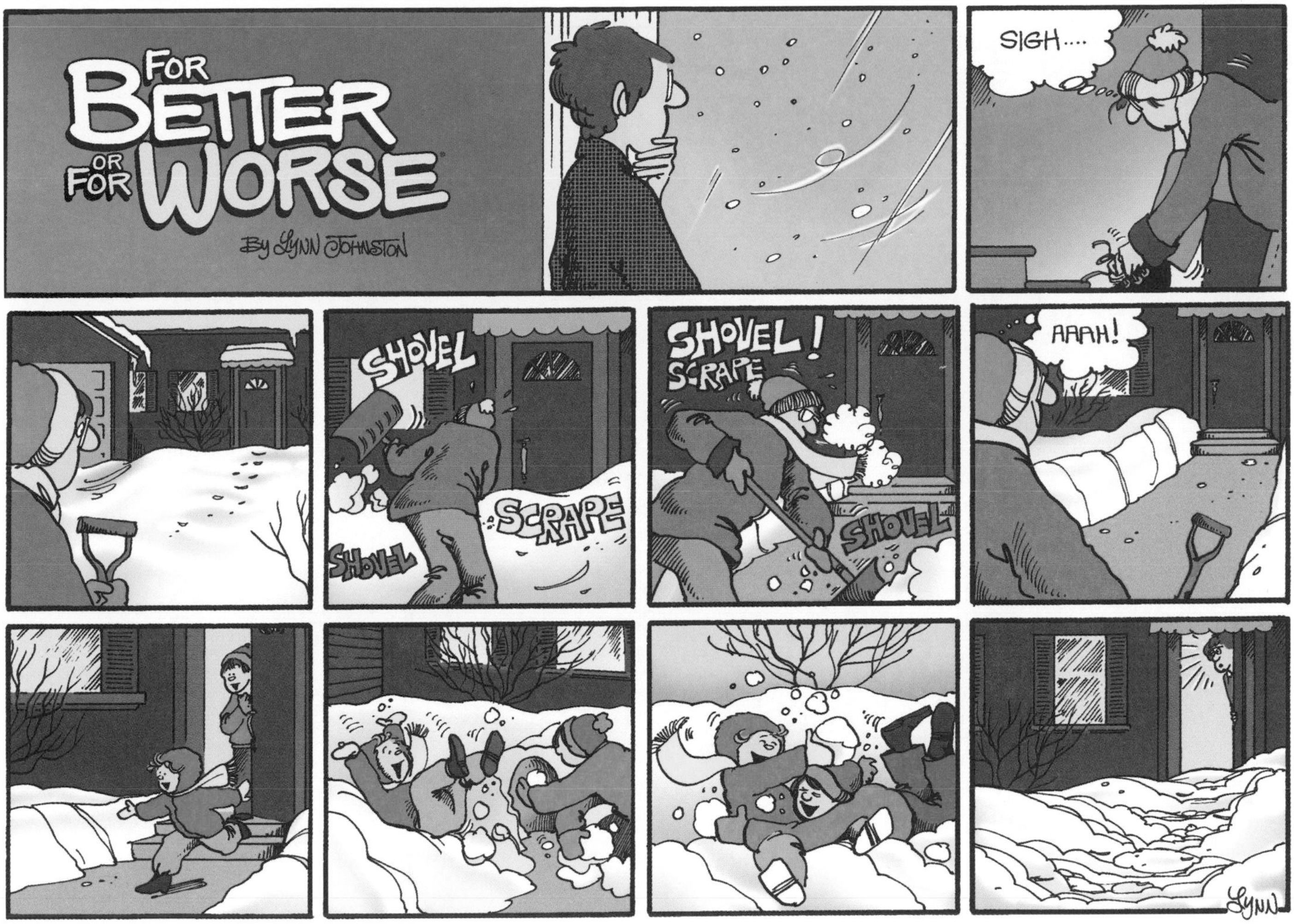
FOR BETTER OR FOR WORSE
BY LYNN JOHNSTON
SIGH....
SHOVEL
SCRAPE
SHOVEL
SHOVEL!
SCRAPE
SHOVEL
AAAH!
LYNN

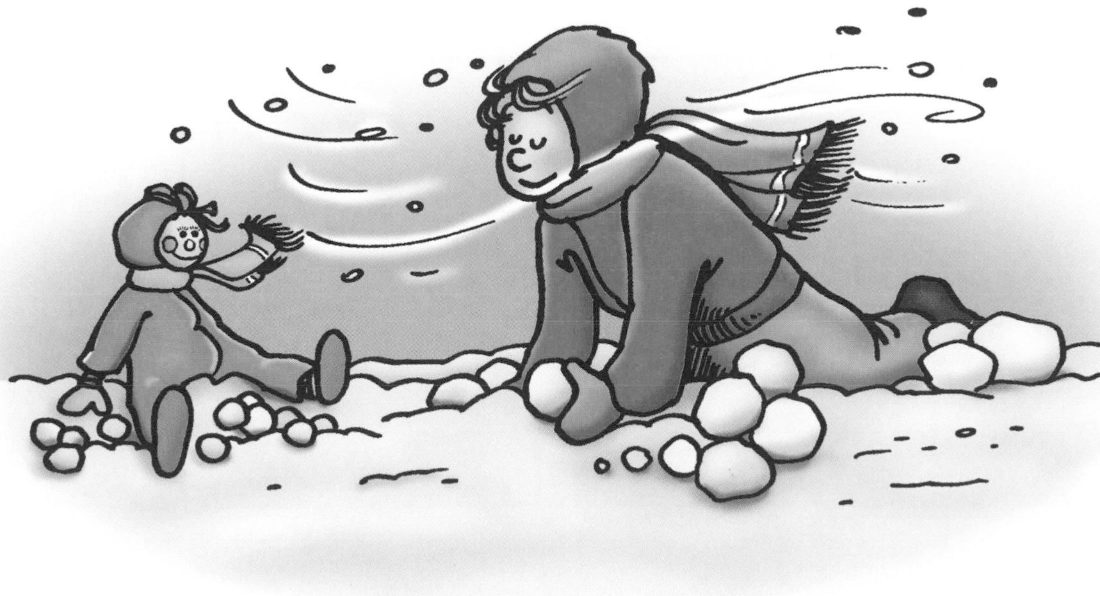

SO - TELL ME, ELLY - WHAT'S HAPPENING BETWEEN TED AND CONNIE?

OH, ANNE - HERE WE ARE AGAIN - GOSSIPING ABOUT POOR CONNIE.

IT'S NOT GOSSIP, ELLY! WE CARE ABOUT HER! WE UNDERSTAND HER! WE'RE HER BEST FRIENDS!

NOW! GIMME THE DIRT!

I don't think my friends and I gossiped like this about anyone. We certainly talked about our friends with concern and sometimes curiosity, but we were there for each other and cared too much to trivialize any news we did have to share. In this panel, I've shown Annie to be uncaring and sensationalistic. I don't know anybody who is this superficial — I did this story to give the strip some bite!

ELLY - IF TED IS STILL BEING A JERK···· WHY DOESN'T CONNIE JUST KISS HIM GOODBYE?

SHE FIGURES HE'LL CHANGE, I GUESS. WITH ENOUGH TALKING AND UNDERSTANDING, THINGS WILL WORK OUT.

TROUBLE IS, SHE'S DOING ALL THE TALKING AND UNDERSTANDING.

Having been there and done that, I no longer wonder why people in miserable relationships stay together. For every reason to break away, there is usually an equally compelling reason to stay together, be it children, financial dependency, or the hope that one more kick at the can will resolve things. No relationship is all bad — some are worth fighting for. Being alone after a rocky relationship might sound like freedom, but it's not — sometimes you are better off with the devil you know.

MOM? YOU HAFTA GO OUT AGAIN?

I'M GOING TO ANOTHER LIBRARY MEETING, ELIZABETH. IT'S IMPORTANT.

MORE 'PORTANT THAN ME?

NOW AN' THEN ···· I HIT HER WITH A GOOD ONE!

I travelled for work more than I needed to. I kept a suitcase partially packed, and I accepted everything from book signings to speaking engagements, thinking it was something I had to do. With great babysitters nearby and in-laws down the road, I didn't feel too guilty about leaving. In truth, the travelling was selfishly for me — I needed to get away. From time to time, Aaron and Kate pointed this out with great clarity.

I cannot stress enough how important it is to volunteer. My dad used to say, "You pay for an education, don't you? Well, working for free is a great education!" It's true. You learn new skills, meet new people, and gain respect for having done a job well — all for the personal rewards it brings AND for a good, credible, enthusiastic reference. Sounds corny, but every good job I have ever had was granted to me because I was recommended by someone for whom I had worked for free!

This is how I felt when I got my job with McMaster University. It was a job that required all the skills I was born with and more. As a medical artist, I could make use of every resource I had — from my days at the animation studio in Vancouver to my art school anatomy classes. I was fascinated by everything medical and was about to be given an open door into any area I wished to explore. I was beyond happy! This same feeling came again years later when I began my career in the comics.

We would never identify the good times as being good if we didn't have crap to compare them with. There's no way Heaven could be perfect bliss, because we wouldn't appreciate it! Humans need the rollercoaster of ups and downs — which is why we continue to make life so darned difficult for ourselves!

Panel 1:
SO-YOU'VE GOT A JOB!!

YEAH! AN' EVEN JOHN LIKES THE IDEA!

Panel 2:
I GUESS HE FIGURES IT'LL BE A GOOD OPPORTUNITY FOR YOU!

Panel 3:
NO, HE FIGURES MY SALARY WILL COVER THE MORTGAGE.

There's nothing more boring in the comics than talking heads, so in order to make this bit of dialogue more interesting, I had Elly and Connie working out at the gym. This trick also gave me an opportunity to get the characters out of the house and to draw them in action!

Panel 1:
WHAT WILL YOU BE DOING FOR THE LIBRARY ANYWAYS, EL?

Panel 2:
OH, ORGANIZING PUPPET SHOWS, CHILDREN'S FILMS, WORKSHOPS....

Panel 3:
WE'LL BE LENDING VIDEO CASSETTES, PROMOTING LIVE THEATRE....

Panel 4:
DOESN'T ANYBODY READ ANY MORE?

I received a number of complaints from librarians who thought I was trivializing their jobs by suggesting that anyone could just walk into a library and get hired. This story was based on the Dundas Public Library, which was always looking for volunteers. These complaints gave me reason to look into the credentials required to become a librarian, and I was impressed by the qualifications required to achieve this difficult degree! As someone who loved literature and had hoped for a writing career, I thought a volunteer position at the local library was a perfect fit for Elly Patterson.

I have to tell you a story here. I was on a book tour, travelling through the United States. I was checking into a hotel in Chicago when a group of ladies ran through the lobby, laughing uproariously and having a ball. "There's a convention going on," the clerk at the desk told me. "This is the noisiest, most party-loving group of people I have ever seen!" "Wow," I replied. "Are they in sports? Theatre?" "No," the young lady answered, "they're librarians!"

WE'VE BEEN EXER-CISING FOR 3 WEEKS NOW, ELLY. FEEL ANY DIFFERENCE?

YEAH! I THINK I'VE LOST A BIT OF WEIGHT AROUND MY-UH......

WHAT'S THAT?

...A COUPLE OF WADDED UP KLEENEXES.

I THOUGHT THEY WERE HIPS.

DON'T GO STRAIGHT HOME, ELLY.... COME IN FOR A WHILE!

THE PLACE IS A WRECK! I'VE BEEN WORKING DAY SHIFT ALL WEEK.

TED'S HERE, BUT HE JUST DOESN'T SEEM TO BE ABLE TO DO HOUSE-WORK.

HOWCOME A MAN WITH 4 UNIVERSITY DEGREES CAN'T FIGURE OUT THE KNOBS ON A DISH-WASHER

SLAM!!

HARK.... THE LIGHT OF MY LIFE RETURNETH....

I WAS OVER AT CONNIE'S AND RIGHT IN THE MIDDLE OF OUR CONVERSATION, TED YAWNS AND ASKS WHEN I'M LEAVING!!

KNOW WHAT I DID? I GOT UP, PUT ON MY COAT AND LEFT! THAT'S WHAT I DID !!!

TED'S METHODS WERE ALWAYS CRASS ....BUT EFFECTIVE.

My affinity for the art of George Booth comes out in the way I draw interaction between people and pets; George was able to make the funniest statements with body language and a simple, knowing glance. Although I only met him once, he has been one of my best teachers!

Lynn Lake, as I have said so many times, did not have the warmest climate. On the rare occasion that Katie did want to wear a dress, it was often too cold to go outside in one. At one point, Kate was determined to wear a pretty summer dress she'd been given. I let her do it. Fortunately, it fit over a warm sweater and her winter snow pants!

....MAKE 'ER NICE AN' SOLID SO'S NOBODY CAN KNOCK 'ER OVER!

OK- NOW CUT SOME NOTCHES HERE-SO'S WE CAN SEE WHO'S COMIN' BY!

MORE SNOWBALLS, GUYS! WE GOTTA GET MORE SNOWBALLS!!

OH....UH— HI, DADDY!

WHAT MAKES YOU THINK WE WERE GONNA THROW THESE AT ANYBODY?!

When it did snow, the stuff that fell on North Vancouver was perfect for forts and fighting. It was sticky and heavy and packed well. As soon as there was enough of it, forts would go up in minutes. My dad loved to make snow forts. He taught us to make the base wider than the next layer, and he was strong enough to lift the heaviest blocks into place for us. After the fort was built, of course, we needed ammo, and after the ammo was piled, we needed an enemy! This is where my brother came in. Dad would build two forts and was the perfect mercenary — he fought for both sides.

There were four boys in the neighbourhood who were regular chums of Alan's. I had, perhaps, three friends willing to go head-to-head with the opposition, and the fight would begin. Ducking, hiding, running, and throwing, we'd batter each other and Dad with hard, icy, wet snow, which stung as it splattered against our jackets, hats, and faces. We got soaked! I remember being so cold that my fingers felt like bones rattling against skin and my feet ceased to feel anything. We quit only when we were cold and exhausted, and a winner was declared.

Our house was heated by a wood and coal furnace. Mom would hang our wet clothes over the vents and make us all hot chocolate. We'd huddle under warm blankets, and dry socks were handed out all 'round. Having been enemies a few minutes beforehand, the two sides recuperated in comfort, happily sharing the same space.

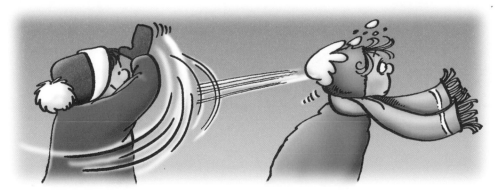

ELLY, ARE YOU FINISHED IN THE BATHROOM YET?

USE THE ONE DOWNSTAIRS.

I CAN'T-ALL MY STUFF IS IN THAT ONE !!!

JOHN-IF I'M GOING TO BE WORKING-WE'LL HAVE TO SHARE THIS BATHROOM IN THE MORNING.

THIS ISN'T SHARING -THIS IS SACRIFICE !!

YOU GOTTA GO TO WORK TODAY, DON'T YOU, MOM.

UH-HUH.

I THOUGHT SO.

YOU LOOK NICE FOR A CHANGE !

Working at home meant that I could wear anything. I was usually in jeans and a sweater when my day began. After a few years of this kind of garb, I began to envy the ladies who actually dressed up for work, whose wardrobe was current and whose appearance was groomed. When I complimented them on their attire and told them I wished I had an excuse like they did to get out of the house and wear nice clothing every day, I discovered that they envied ME!

ELLY'S WORKING IS SURE GOING TO CHANGE THINGS AROUND OUR PLACE, JEAN.

THIS MORNING, SHE TOOK OFF AT 8:30. -I HAD TO MAKE MY OWN LUNCH !

TAKE A LOOK AT MY FACE, DOC... CAN YOU SEE THE DEEP SYMPATHY WRITTEN ON IT?

NO.

EXACTLY !

IT'S FANTASTIC, JOHN! -I GO IN 3 MORNINGS A WEEK-AND A LOT OF THE WORK I CAN DO AT HOME.

-THEY EVEN SAID I COULD BRING ELIZABETH WITH ME IF I HAD TO!

TAKE A KID TO WORK? -ARE THEY ALL NUTS?

NO...

THEY'RE ALL MOTHERS.

TOMORROW, I'M STARTING A STORY HOUR FOR PRE-SCHOOLERS.

I NEVER EXPECTED YOU TO BE INTERESTED IN WORKING WITH KIDS, ELLY!

THAT'S CRAZY! I LOVE KIDS! I GET ALONG FINE WITH THEM!

...AS LONG AS THEY'RE NOT HER OWN!

JOHN, I'M SO EXCITED ABOUT THE LIBRARY JOB! IT'S A WHOLE BRAND NEW DOOR OPENING UP!

YOU'RE NOT ANGRY, ARE YOU?

NO. I GUESS I'M JEALOUS.

I USED TO LIKE WORKING .... ONCE.

59

JOHN... HAVE I TOLD YOU LATELY HOW MUCH I APPRECIATE YOU?

YOU'RE THOUGHTFUL AND UNDERSTANDING AND... MMMMMM

WHAT ARE THEY DOING —VALENTINE'S DAY ISN'T 'TILL NEXT WEEK!

MAYBE THEY'RE PRACTICING!

HEY! MIKE! IT'S DEANNA SOBINSKI!

GIGGLE!

SMIRK! GUFFAW!

CUT IT OUT, GUYS - JUST QUIT IT!!

HEY, DEANNA - IT'S YOUR LOV-MMMPH!!!

I HATE DEANNA SOBINSKI!!

At school, Aaron was constantly being asked, "Who is Deanna Sobinski?" He didn't have a girlfriend that I knew of, and there were no other Deannas in town except for my friend's daughter — who was about the same age as Kate. It was assumed that everything I wrote was directly related to my family. Because of this, many storylines were hard on my kids — especially anything to do with childhood sweethearts! Despite my explanations, some folks still believe the strip is autobiographical.

BOY, YOU DIDN'T HAFTA SAY YOU HATED DEANNA, MAN!

I DON'T HATE HER! YOU'RE JUST ALWAYS BUGGING ME - AN' I SAID IT, THAT'S ALL!

BOY, LOOKIT HER GO!

YEAH! IS SHE MAD!

(SIGH)... IT MUST BE NICE TO BE POPULAR.

I have to give credit to one of Aaron's teachers for this punch line. Sheena told me that when one of her kindergarten students was severely ill, her class was comforted to see that her seat was still there. As long as her place in the class remained, they knew she was coming back.

We gave Aaron a key to the house, hoping he wouldn't lose it. He did. The key was as much of a concern to him as his glasses, which he hated to wear. He lost them, he broke them, and he left them at home. The frustration his glasses caused was part of the reason why they never appeared in the strip! When he was finally old enough for contacts, he was overjoyed. Now that I too have to wear glasses, I can see how hard it was for an active, conservative kid to accept them.

FOR BETTER OR FOR WORSE

By Lynn Johnston

HEY, MOM! I BROUGHT A FEW OF THE GUYS IN TO SEE THE NEW VIDEO GAMES!

WHAT'S WITH YOU, ELLY? YOU LOOK AWFUL!

THANKS.

FIRST, THE SANDER YOU ORDERED ARRIVED.... THEN PHIL AND GEORGIA STOPPED IN FOR COFFEE....

—THREE KIDS FROM THE HOCKEY TEAM CAME BY SELLING CHOCOLATES...

ANNIE CAME OVER WITH A NEIGHBOR WHO'S JUST MOVED IN DOWN THE STREET...

—AND ON TOP OF IT ALL— MICHAEL'S GOT THE REC-ROOM FULL OF FRIENDS!!

WHY DID EVERYONE HAVE TO SHOW UP TODAY OF ALL DAYS?!!

WHAT'S SO SPECIAL ABOUT TODAY?

I DECIDED NOT TO GET DRESSED..

Lynn

In Vancouver during the fifties, there was a popular children's radio show called *Kiddie's Carnival*. It was done in a small studio with a live audience, which you could be part of by writing into the program and asking for tickets. It was first write, first served. My mom managed to score two of them. Not only did she and I have tickets, but we were told that I would get to be one of the children allowed to say "hello" on *Kiddie's Carnival* radio! It was an exciting day. I had never been in a radio station before, and when it was my turn to go up to the microphone, I was terrified. The host was reassuring. He moved the big silver microphone right under my nose and said, "Lynn, it's your turn to say hello! Who would you like to say hello to today?" Meanwhile, my dad was at work. He had the radio on, and everyone in Shores Jewellery was listening. Sweating and shaking, I leaned into the mic and said, "Hello, Grandma and Grandpa!" Dad was crushed. He had expected me to say hello to him. I wasn't thinking. I just blurted out the first thing that came to mind. When he got home later that evening, it was clear that I had let him down. Mom thought it was nice that I had thought of her parents, though, and decided to call them and ask what they thought of the broadcast. Sadly, they hadn't been listening. To this day, I think about that missed opportunity, and I wish that I'd acknowledged the one person to whom it really mattered.

LOOK AT ALL THE VALENTINES! ... WHO'S THIS ONE FOR?

OH, I DUNNO ... SOMEBODY, I GUESS. HAVEN'T FIGURED OUT WHO. JUST— SOMEBODY.

for Deanna...

Valentines came in big plastic bags when I was a kid. We'd get perhaps 25 pretty little cards for a few dollars, and we'd give one to everyone in our class. This meant that we all came home with a fistful of valentines. Nobody was left out. It was tradition. In grade one, I had a crush on a boy named Jimmy Thompson. I was crazy about him until Valentine's Day, when I gave him a card, but he didn't give a card to anyone. I was hurt — I never knew that his family just couldn't afford them.

THANKS FOR THE NICE VALENTINE, MICHAEL.

UH?

I NEVER SIGNED IT. HOW'D YOU KNOW IT WAS FROM ME?

WELL—WHEN I FOUND IT ON MY DESK—AN' OPENED IT UP.....

... YOU WERE THE ONLY ONE WATCHING!

HEY, DID YOU GIVE A VALENTINE TO DEANNA SOBINSKI?

WOW! WAIT 'TILL THE GUYS HEAR THIS!!

YAAH! MICHAEL LOVES DEANNA! MICHAEL LOVES DEANNA!!

TSK. THEY'RE SUCH CHILDREN.

WHY AREN'T YOU WATCHING TV WITH DADDY?

HE SAID THERE WAS TOO MUCH SEX AND VIOLENCE—AN' HE TOLD US TO LEAVE.

WHAT'S HE WATCHING—SOME GRADE Z MOVIE?

NO. THE NEWS.

MOM—DID YOU EVER REALLY "LIKE" SOMEONE WHEN YOU WERE IN SCHOOL?

SURE. I HAD A CRUSH ON ONE GUY FOR 3 WHOLE YEARS!

HOW COME THEY CALL IT A "CRUSH?"

MAYBE 'CAUSE THAT'S WHAT HAPPENS TO YOUR FEELINGS WHEN THEY FIND OUT!

YES—I USED TO WRITE VERY AFFECTIONATE NOTES TO THIS BOY WHEN I WAS IN SCHOOL…

…THEN HE'D SHOW THEM TO HIS FRIENDS …. AND THEY'D ALL LAUGH.

THEN THEY'D TEASE ME.

YEAH. I KNOW WHAT YOU MEAN.

NEVER PUT ANYTHING IN WRITING.

In junior high school, I had a crush on a boy named Calvin. He delivered the newspaper on Fifth Street. I'd delay going home until he had picked up his papers and I could walk with him. I wrote him a love note one day and pressed it into his hand as we left our class. I was jittery with emotion. I thought he would treasure it. I was shocked to find out that he'd read it aloud to his friends during lunch hour. Betrayal like that should have killed the crush … but it lasted a whole three years!

Everyone smoked when I was a kid. It was cool to have a cigarette in your mouth — you looked like a movie star. At the corner store we could buy packets of candy cigarettes. They were sticky and gritty and tasted vaguely like peppermint. If it was cold enough outside, our breath turned to steam, and we'd pretend we were lighting up for real. When my brother and I finally scored the real thing, I was surprised to discover how horrible they were. How anyone gets hooked is beyond me!

This video arcade was based on Fergy's corner store in Lynn Lake as well as an arcade in downtown North Bay. Fergy's was off limits because the tough kids hung out there, played pool, and smoked. The arcade in North Bay, on the other hand, was a great place for kids to experience all of the latest video games and get some of the craze out of their systems. I have to admit — I was as fascinated by them as they were, and I encouraged them to play so that I could watch!

I had a couple of friends who were latchkey kids. Their parents worked, and after work they'd spend time at the bar before going home. Both girls were the guardians of younger siblings. They literally raised their brothers and sisters because their parents were never home. I remember being jealous of my friends' freedom. We played house. We'd put the little ones to bed and pretend we were grownups. For me, it was a wonderful game ... but later I could go home and be a kid again.

The kids were never far away — I used to listen to their banter as they made up games, created forts in the living room, and played house. I was impressed by their ability to fantasize. I remembered my own childhood, when a mud pie tasted like the real thing, and if you rolled up in a blanket, you could fly. Even though we seemed to be in a world of our own, we were still aware of our immediate environment.

Aaron, Katie, and Aaron's friend Roy were playing one day, and some of their dialogue disturbed me — they were talking about bombs, murder, divorce, and other things they had heard about on television. This had to be absorbed, of course, and dealt with as much as any other experience outside of *Sesame Street* and Saturday morning cartoons. I worried that I was not talking to my kids enough. Later, when Roy had gone home, I asked them about their conversations, their ideas, and their perceptions. I felt good about being there to answer questions and explain some facts. In return, Aaron asked me if life was the same for me when I was a kid, and I had to say that it was — we just didn't hear or see as much as they do now. We were far more protected from negative realities. When I think about it, we were really naïve, and for that, I'm somewhat grateful!

I now have a grandchild. I see kids as young as two happily using computers, eBooks, and iPads, and I wonder how much more the babies of today are learning … too soon, too fast.

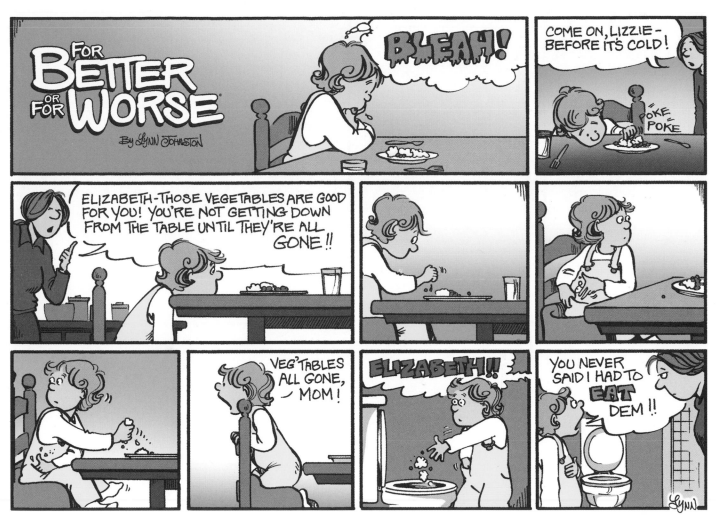

There was a law in our house: If you didn't like what was on your plate, it didn't matter — you had to eat it all. This rule was enforced unless we were too sick to sit there or were absent altogether! My brother, Alan, was always trying to escape the likes of cold creamed peas, canned corned beef, or liver in gravy. He would hide a wad in his pockets or the cuffs of his pants and, convincingly full, would leave the table. Once he was being so gross at dinnertime, he was sent to his room to eat. He went happily and returned minutes later with a suspiciously empty plate. He said he had eaten everything, but there was evidence to the contrary; the gravy was scraped to the side of the plate, and the toilet had just been flushed. With her hands on her hips, Mom accused him of lying, but he stuck to his story. It was his word against the gravy. She gave him "the glare," but he stared her down. Mom dragged Alan to the biff. She wanted to scope out the scene of the crime but found nothing to pin on him. The gravy trail was the only real evidence, the one thing that could trip him up. With Alan's ear between her thumb and forefingers, she marched him brusquely back into the kitchen to resume her interrogation … and found our dad happily washing the dishes. The accused's plate was clean. From that day on, the rule was altered to allow for differences in tastes and appetites. Once again, Alan had defied our mom, and Dad was a hero. Until then, even HE had to eat stuff he hated!

When I moved to Hamilton, Ontario, from Vancouver, British Columbia, I was barely 22 and very innocent. Despite my art school experience during the hippie movement, with its free love and smokable happiness, I had seen and tried very little. I joined Vic Tanny's health club with a friend, and when I saw several naked older women enjoying the hot tub, I was both appalled and curious. I had never seen anything like this. It was fascinating. We all really do come in different shapes and sizes.

Dear me. Here is another strip that got me into hot water. Readers thought John had actually KICKED the dog in panel two! What I had tried to show was John putting his foot under Farley's rump and moving him. I would never have shown someone kicking a dog! This taught me to never draw an action unless I could draw it well!

At this time in the evolution of the strip, I decided to have Mike's friend, Gordon, be a bit of a negative force. In my mind, all of the auxiliary characters were becoming clear and defined, and it seemed right for Gordon Mayes to have some baggage. Something in his life made him cynical and tougher than the other kids, but I hadn't yet figured out what it was. It sounds unbelievable, but these characters evolved on their own. In a way, they told me who they were and how they lived.

72

Remember eating snow and believing it tasted like ice cream? If you don't, you didn't grow up in a northern climate! The only snow we didn't eat was yellow!

Although we tried not to talk "baby talk" to the kids, we adored the words they made up themselves.

From time to time, I confess, we did speak to them in their native tongue.

Farley, the real dog, hated baths. If he just heard the word, he'd head for the hills. I usually washed him outside, but during the winter I would stuff him into the tub, which meant the entire bathroom got wet along with him. After I dried and brushed him, Farley looked like a massive plush toy, his fur poofing out as if he'd stuck his tail in a light socket. He would look like this until he had to go outside, where he'd find something dirty to roll in. He was a lot of work, but I didn't mind. He was family … and a real character!

Loretta and Gail are the names of two Lynn Lake friends. I used their names here just to have some fun. The trouble was that the real Loretta looked so much like Connie Porrier (Elly Patterson's neighbour and good friend) that I literally drew two Connies! The artist who was helping me with the colouring knew Loretta. She became confused and gave "Connie," who was seated, dark hair and made the arriving "Loretta" blonde — which in real life she is. In order to keep continuity and separate two characters, which had been drawn so alike, we had to make the character Connie blonde and my friend Loretta dark. Still with me? My friend Loretta was now unrecognizable in the strip. A better artist might have been able to draw the two sufficiently well to have avoided this conundrum altogether. I am often asked to do caricatures, and this is why I turn folks down!

Monique was a sweet young woman who won a trip to Lynn Lake to meet me, on a show called *Thrill of a Lifetime*. I was the thrill! Part of the arrangement was that she would see herself in the comic strip and receive an original drawing. Because our encounter had been so short and I had done just one drawing for the show (a Sunday page), I decided to include her as one of the library staff. I never heard from her, but I hoped she enjoyed her brief appearances.

NOW WE HAVE A HAMSTER - CALLED HUMPHREY, YET!!

IT'S ONLY FOR A WEEK, JOHN.

HEY, MOM - WHAT WOULD HAPPEN IF WE GAVE HUMPHREY TO THE DOG?!

IT'S TO TEACH HIM RESPONSIBILITY

SQUEEEEK!!
RATTLE RATTLE
SQUEEK SQUEEK SQUEE

WHAT THE *⊚☆! IS THAT?

IT'S THE HAMSTER. HE'S RUNNING ON HIS WHEEL.

SQUEEK!

HE'S NOCTURNAL. HE COMES ALIVE AT NIGHT.

RATTLE! RATTLE

NOT IF HE WANTS TO STAY ALIVE 'TILL MORNING.

THERE. I OILED THE WHEEL IN THE HAMSTER CAGE.

GOOD. AS LONG AS HE'S QUIET - HE'LL BE NO TROUBLE AT ALL...

MOM! THE HAMSTER GOTS A BALL HE CAN RUN IN!

MICHAEL'S LETTIN' HIM GO ALL OVER THE HOUSE!

BAM! CRAKKITA POP POP POP BAM!

HE HAS A LITTLE TROUBLE WITH STAIRS!

SHUT THE DOOR QUICK, DADDY! THE HAMSTER'S LOOSE!

PUT THE DOG IN THE GARAGE! I THINK I'VE GOT HIM CORNERED UNDER THE SINK!

HAND ME THE FLASHLIGHT, MICHAEL.

ANY LUCK YET?

MOM, IF I DON'T FIND HUMPHREY-THE WHOLE CLASS WILL HATE ME!

DON'T WORRY, HONEY — DADDY WILL CATCH HIM. HE KNOWS WHAT HE'S DOING.

The school hamster did not come to our house, but we did hamster-sit for friends. After a week of sawdust, nocturnal scuffling, an escape into the back of the couch, and the omnipresent rodent smell, I was pleased to return the animal to his rightful home — happy in the knowledge that we would never own one ourselves.

Canadian Gulf Delta Sierra Tango were the identification letters on the side of our last aircraft: CGDST. This was shortened to "Delta Sierra Tango" when we identified ourselves to the tower for take-offs, landings, and just checking in. DST was a beautiful Navajo, which seated six people and could carry two more if we took out the small portable toilet and the storage cabinet. We had owned various aircraft over the years, but this was a commercial plane, which had been built as a medevac: a rescue craft with an extra door to accommodate stretchers and medical equipment. This was our magic carpet. It could go anywhere! It was equipped with oxygen, which meant we could cross the country at higher altitudes — going over the Rockies safely and easily, avoiding the passes and the turbulence around the peaks.

From the windows of DST, we saw most of Canada and the United States. Rod was an excellent pilot who took no chances; he knew all too well that pilot error was responsible for most airplane accidents. Despite our love of flying, a few years after we moved to northern Ontario, we decided to sell the plane. It became too costly to maintain, and we really didn't need it as much as we did up north. At the time, I was doing a lot of travel for business, and North Bay has an excellent airport. It was much easier to jump on a commercial flight, which made it hard to justify owning such a fast and fancy machine.

I worked hard to get my pilot's licence with the intention of eventually buying another aircraft, but we never did. I'm sad to see this chapter in my life over — we had some great adventures. In my next life, I'm gonna fly again!

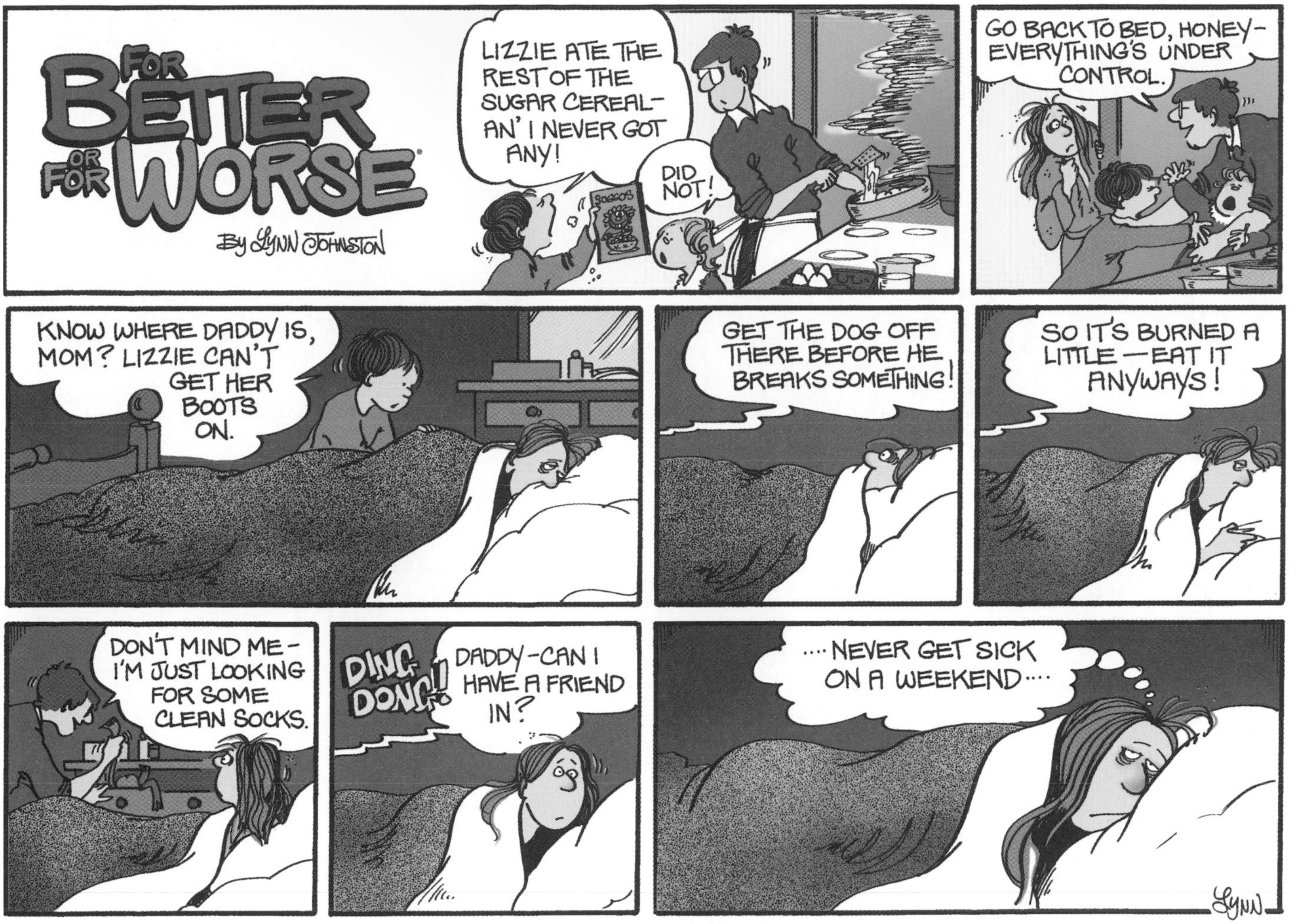
FOR BETTER OR FOR WORSE
BY LYNN JOHNSTON
LIZZIE ATE THE REST OF THE SUGAR CEREAL- AN' I NEVER GOT ANY!
DID NOT!
GO BACK TO BED, HONEY- EVERYTHING'S UNDER CONTROL.
KNOW WHERE DADDY IS, MOM? LIZZIE CAN'T GET HER BOOTS ON.
GET THE DOG OFF THERE BEFORE HE BREAKS SOMETHING!
SO IT'S BURNED A LITTLE — EAT IT ANYWAYS!
DON'T MIND ME- I'M JUST LOOKING FOR SOME CLEAN SOCKS.
DING DONG!!
DADDY-CAN I HAVE A FRIEND IN?
....NEVER GET SICK ON A WEEKEND....
LYNN

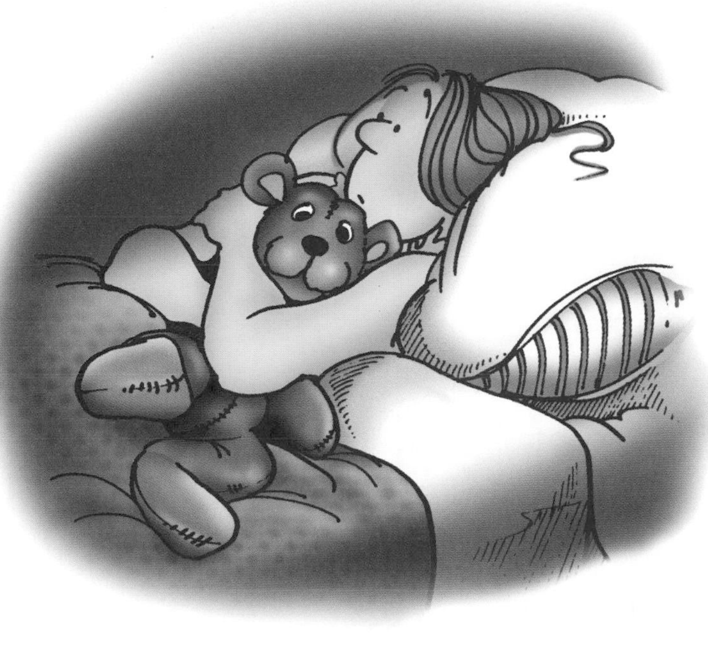

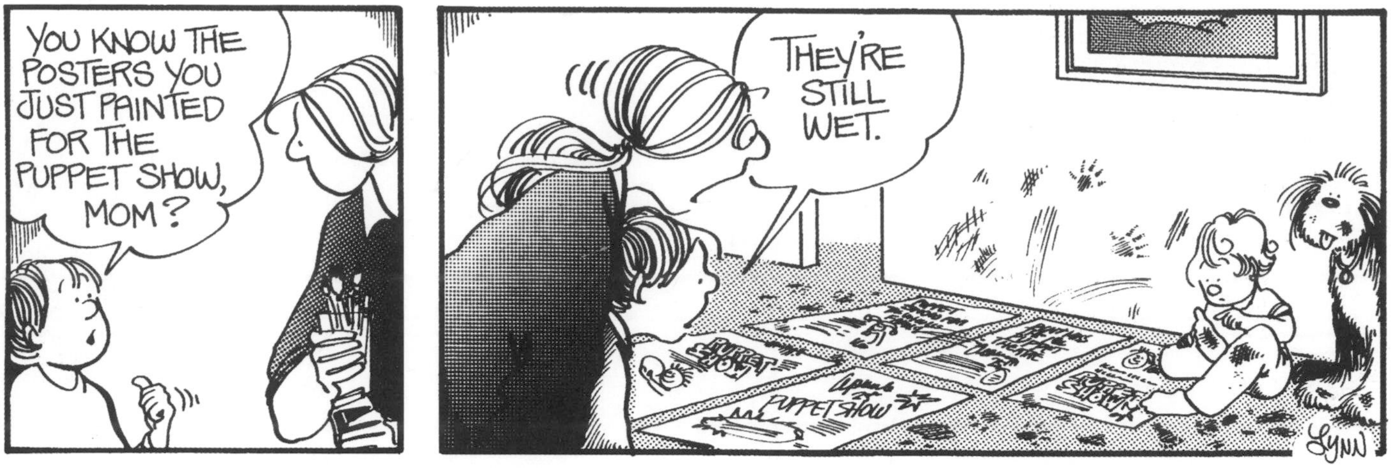
YOU KNOW THE POSTERS YOU JUST PAINTED FOR THE PUPPET SHOW, MOM?
THEY'RE STILL WET.
PUPPET SHOW
LYNN

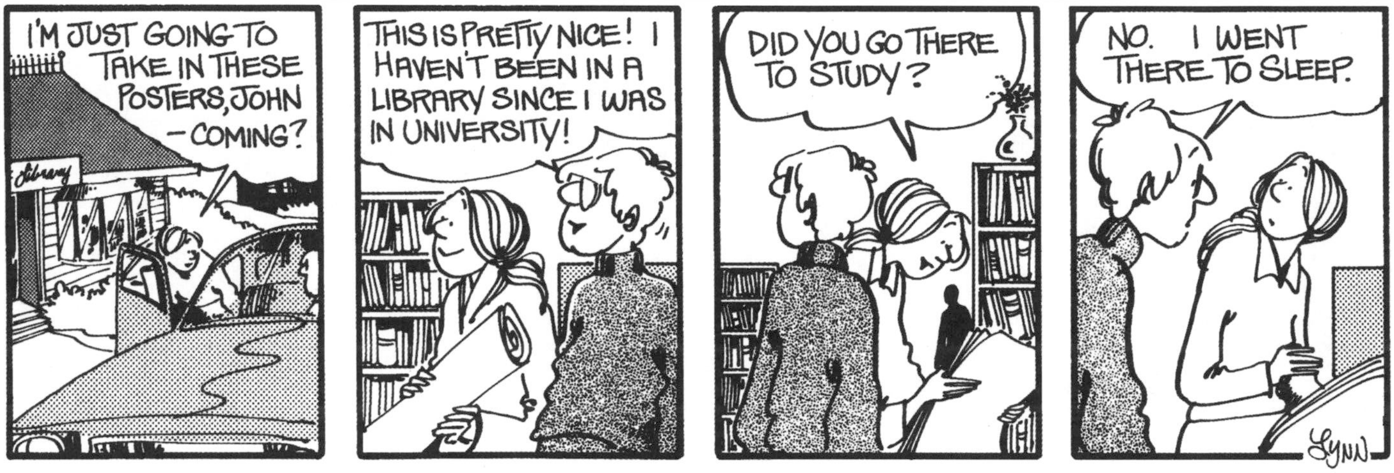
I'M JUST GOING TO TAKE IN THESE POSTERS, JOHN – COMING?
Library
THIS IS PRETTY NICE! I HAVEN'T BEEN IN A LIBRARY SINCE I WAS IN UNIVERSITY!
DID YOU GO THERE TO STUDY?
NO. I WENT THERE TO SLEEP.
LYNN

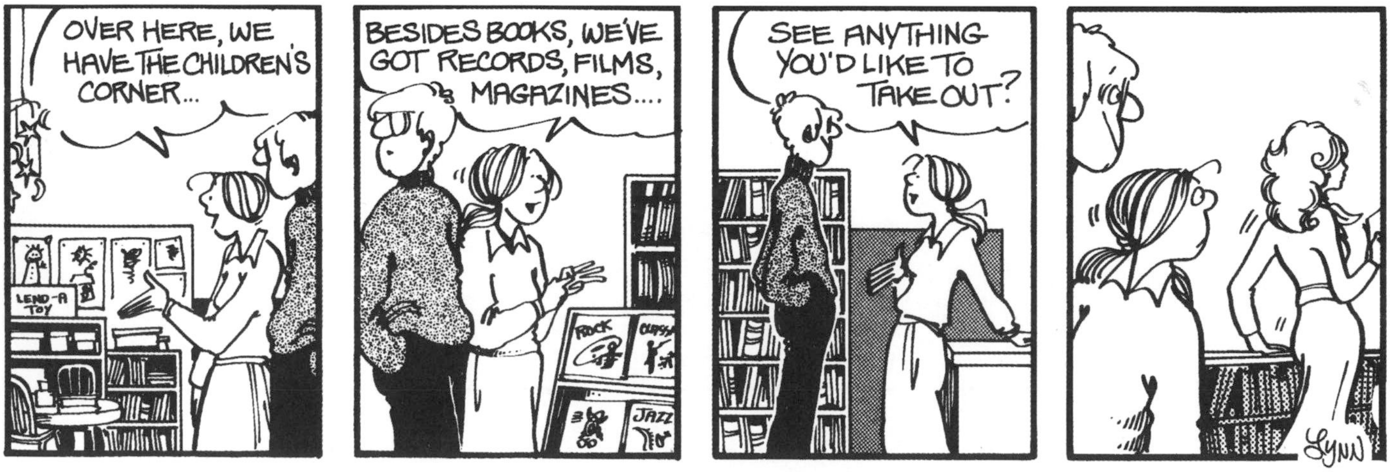
OVER HERE, WE HAVE THE CHILDREN'S CORNER...
LEND-A TOY
BESIDES BOOKS, WE'VE GOT RECORDS, FILMS, MAGAZINES....
ROCK
JAZZ
SEE ANYTHING YOU'D LIKE TO TAKE OUT?
LYNN

Aaron was at least eight before we would leave him at home on his own. We never left him for long — just an hour, perhaps. He always knew where we were, and it was a way to show him that he had our trust. We were able to do this because we had grandparents nearby and neighbours who knew everything that Aaron was up to … and would tell!

I have always been grateful that I learned how to drive standard. If you can use a gear shift, you can drive anything with ease and confidence. Driving standard has allowed me to drive trucks and tractors, a swather, and a combine and also helped me learn how to fly a plane. Using both feet while driving a standard gives you a sort of rhythm, which you need when operating a craft that moves forward, sideways, up, and down — sometimes all at once!

The last standard I owned was a Subaru WRX — a racing-style hatchback with one of those fancy air intakes on the hood that gives your engine extra guts when you need 'em. The first time I drove it, I hit a straight stretch on the highway and just let 'er rip. I had no idea how fast I was going, I just passed everyone in my way … watching their stunned reactions as I whizzed by. In no time there were flashing lights in my rear-view mirror and I was pulled to the side of the road by a serious looking officer. I was admonished for my stupidity and given a hefty fine. But the worst part was watching the people I had passed now passing me … with satisfied smirks on their faces! I now drive an automatic, use the cruise control, and smile at the guys in their sports cars as they scream past — hoping I'll see them getting a ticket around the next bend!

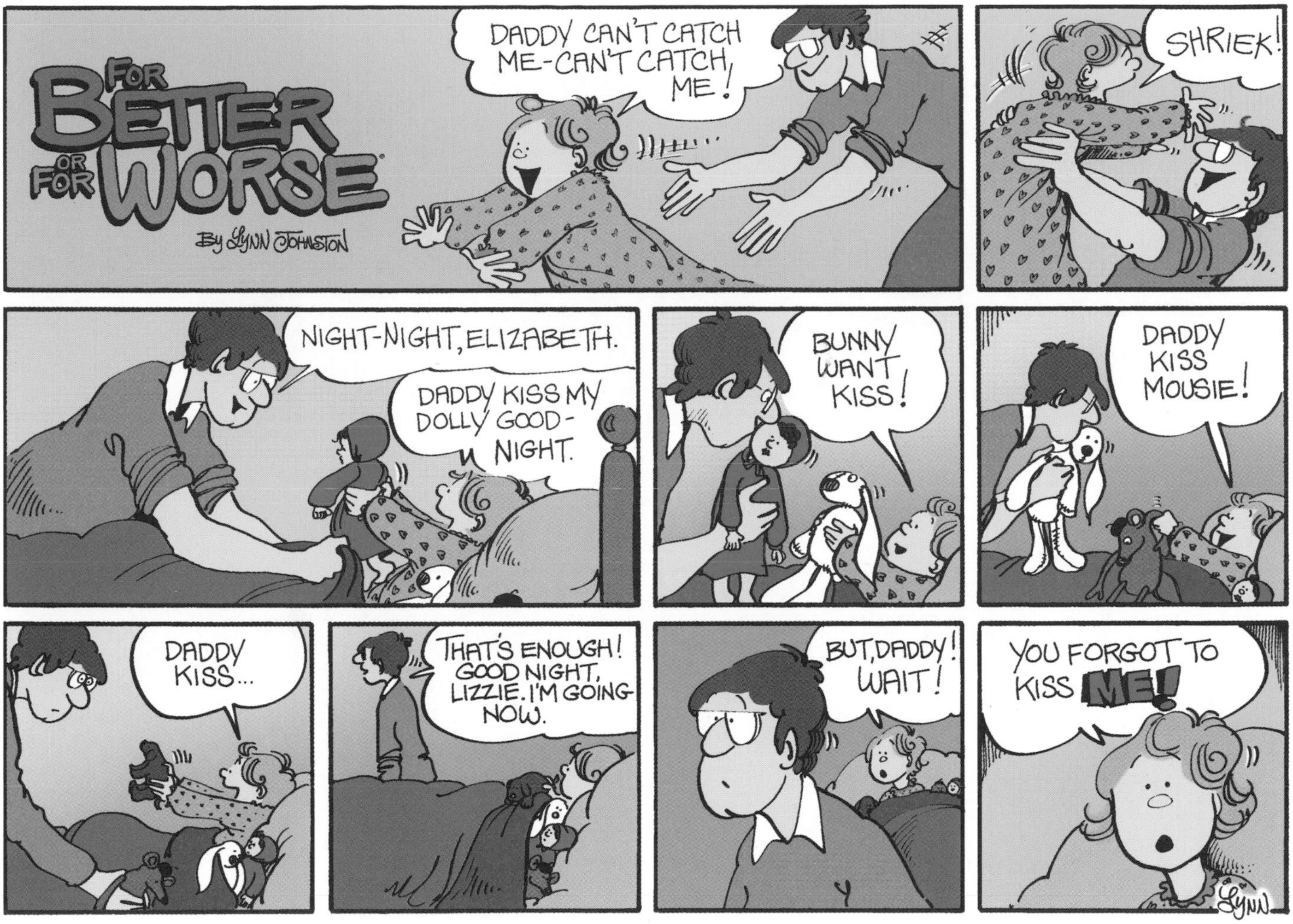

FOR BETTER OR FOR WORSE
BY LYNN JOHNSTON
DADDY CAN'T CATCH ME-CAN'T CATCH ME!
SHRIEK!
NIGHT-NIGHT, ELIZABETH.
DADDY KISS MY DOLLY GOOD-NIGHT.
BUNNY WANT KISS!
DADDY KISS MOUSIE!
DADDY KISS...
THAT'S ENOUGH! GOOD NIGHT, LIZZIE. I'M GOING NOW.
BUT, DADDY! WAIT!
YOU FORGOT TO KISS ME!
LYNN

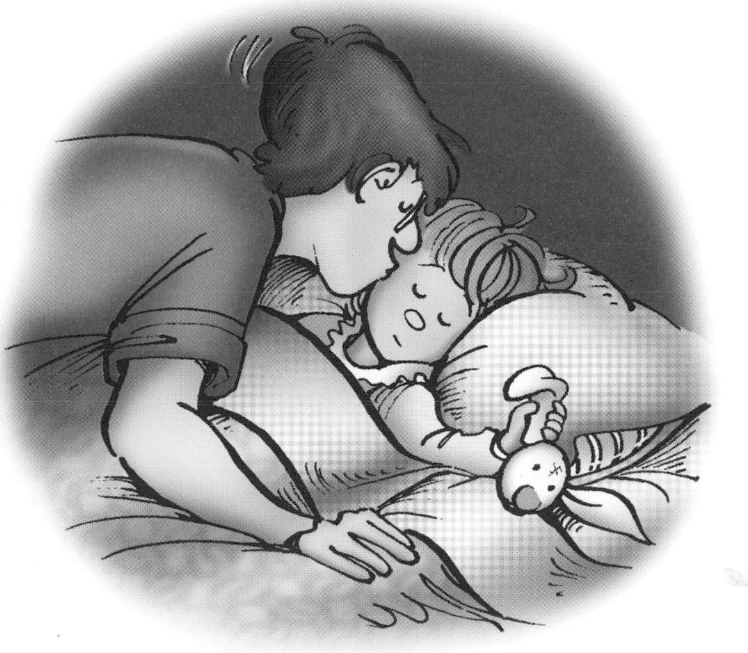

This statement led to several daily strips. Women rarely get to hear this kind of stuff, and I thought it was a nifty insight.

... about this!

This scenario played out between us more than once. It wasn't uncommon for us to deal with the truth in jest.

This was the rule in our house when it came to birthday parties. Although the "rule" was often broken, it did help to reduce the number of kids in attendance.

87

TWIST-TURN-TWIST-TURN AND JUMPING JACKS TO 16 - NOW, CAN-CAN!

IT'S CAN-CAN, MRS. PATTERSON — KEEP IT UP!!

I... (GASP.) CAN'T- CAN'T!!

I was in the best shape ever when I lived in Lynn Lake. The community centre gym was a block away, I walked everywhere, and I was constantly carrying the kids around. There were times when I would carry Katie on my back in a carrier and have Aaron on my hip at the same time. These days, I'm lucky if I can heave a small piece of luggage into an overhead bin!

(GROAN.) WHAT A WORKOUT! THAT INSTRUCTOR IS AMAZING!

I DON'T KNOW HOW ANYBODY CAN KEEP MOVING LIKE THAT AND GIVE ORDERS AT THE SAME TIME!

SHE NEVER SEEMS TO GET TIRED... OR EVEN SHORT OF BREATH!

YEAH. TOO BAD SHE'S SINGLE — SHE'D MAKE A GREAT MOTHER!

WHATCHA DOIN'?

I'M WRITING OUT MY BIRTHDAY PARTY INVITATIONS.

I GET TO COME, YOU KNOW. MOM SAID! YOU SAID NO GIRLS - AN' I'M A GIRL!

THAT'S OK.... YOU'RE INSIGNIFICANT.

DADDY... I'M NOT REALLY SURE... BUT I FINK MICHAEL SWEARED AT ME!

Aaron took a sort of aptitude test one day, and one of the results was that he had an adult vocabulary. This why it was hard to put anything over on him. My brother and I were always encouraged to learn more words; "You can't express yourself properly if you don't have enough words in your head!" was something my mom drilled into us. Aaron had a natural affinity for words and often surprised us with big ones!

This punch line later became the title for a collection book.

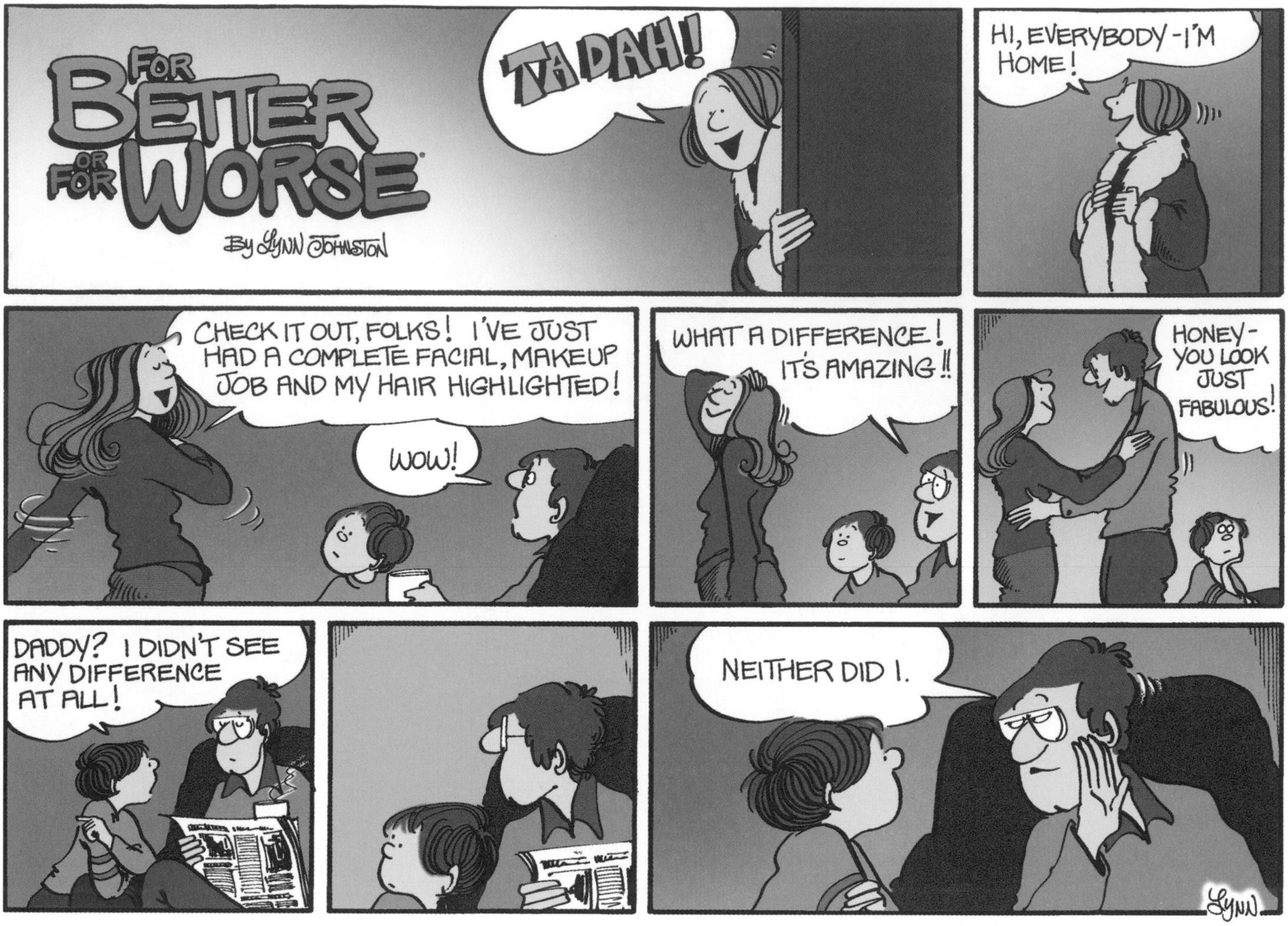
FOR BETTER OR FOR WORSE
By Lynn Johnston
TA DAH!
HI, EVERYBODY - I'M HOME!
CHECK IT OUT, FOLKS! I'VE JUST HAD A COMPLETE FACIAL, MAKEUP JOB AND MY HAIR HIGHLIGHTED!
WOW!
WHAT A DIFFERENCE! IT'S AMAZING!!
HONEY - YOU LOOK JUST FABULOUS!
DADDY? I DIDN'T SEE ANY DIFFERENCE AT ALL!
NEITHER DID I.
LYNN

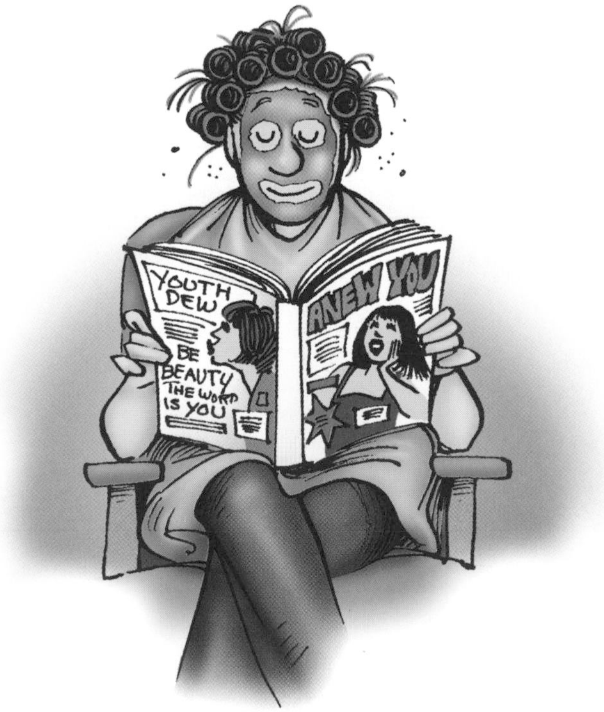
YOUTH DEW
BE BEAUTY THE WORD IS YOU
A NEW YOU

When I look at this now, I smile. I was not yet forty, but I could see myself aging. Every wrinkle was worrisome. The tiniest hint of an eye bag sent me looking for creams. We had been married for a few years and I was wearing some pretty tattered nightgowns. I didn't care much about looking good when I went to bed ... as long as the face looked good in the morning.

Now that I'm 65, I have given up on the face, but I wear pretty nightgowns — I seem to be doing things in reverse!

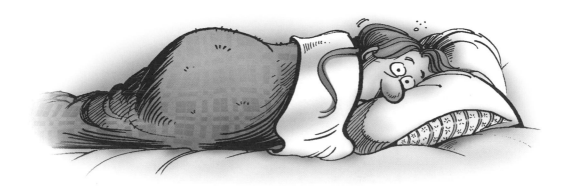

I gave Aaron this lecture and then watched as he welcomed his guests into the house. The first thing they did, of course, was to hand him their gifts so they could take off their shoes and jackets. He grabbed for the gifts and had the last laugh again.

This strip was the catalyst for several letters from post-birthday party moms who wanted to say, "Thanks for telling it like it is." Being able to throw a well-planned kids' party is something moms take pride in, and only WE know how much work it is!

Eldon Park was just down the lane from our house in Lynn Lake. It was a small space; room enough for a roundabout, a slide, and a three-seater swing set. The Kinsmen took care of the grounds and the equipment, and thanks to them, we had an Easter egg hunt each year. It was always a skirmish when the big kids got to the goodies first. Some parents helped the little kids, much to the annoyance of others, but we always managed to escape an altercation. I remember Katie standing by the fence upset because she couldn't find anything. To me, the eggs were visible everywhere, but when I squatted down to her level, I could see what the problem was. Everything was either too high or buried in the grass, which was too tall for her to see over. Sometimes, you really DO have to look at things from your child's point of view!

This is a Vancouver scene. Rain suits were a necessity, and all of us had some kind of plastic or rubberized gear. In high pants and slickers, we'd run around in the rain, jump into puddles, and play in the mud, oblivious to squelching boots, wet mitts, and dripping faces. We would also forget to go to the bathroom, but it hardly mattered: For a moment, we'd be "warm." We west coast kids were part duck when it came to the outdoors. Even a deluge was fun — especially in August. Now, we live in a fairly dry climate where umbrellas are rarely seen and kids won't go out if it's spitting. The other day I was in a children's shop and there was the cutest rain suit I have ever seen. I bought it for my granddaughter, who will soon be walking. Someday, I'm going to put on a raincoat and gum boots and show her what a rainy day is all about!

HOW COME WE GOTTA GO TO UNCLE PHIL'S FOR DINNER?

HE BOUGHT A NEW WOK— AND WANTS TO SHOW IT OFF!

OH.

WHAT DOES "WOK" MEAN?

IT'S ANOTHER WORD FOR "VEGETABLES."

LYNN

....A LITTLE BOK CHOI, SOME GREEN PEPPER, ONION, A TOUCH OF SOYA.....

I LOVE TO COOK, SIS! IT'S LIKE CONDUCTING A SYMPHONY!

IT'S AN ARRANGEMENT OF FLAVORS, COLORS, AROMAS...BLENDING INTO.......

DON'T LOOK NOW, BUT YOU'RE BURNING THE BUTT OFF BEETHOVEN'S 5TH

LYNN

My brother is quite a good cook. He did like to use a wok. Most of the meals he made were in my kitchen, and I still have the wok to prove it!

I REALIZE THERE ARE NO KIDS HERE TO PLAY WITH, MICHAEL.

UNCLE PHIL DOESN'T HAVE ANY TOYS OR COMICS OR GAMES.

BUT, I WANT YOU TO FIND SOMETHING TO DO - UNDERSTAND?

UH HUH.

BOP!

POIT!

LYNN

My first husband was seven years my senior, so quite few of our married friends were older than I and had young families. One young mother was taking an early childhood education class. We'd agreed to meet for coffee afterwards, but she invited me to attend. The speaker was child psychologist. I didn't think he knew what he was talking about. I thought I could teach the class better than he could — and I was the only one in the class without children! Later, my kids made me humble.

Alan did encourage Aaron to play the trumpet. He gave him a few private lessons. The trumpet we had belonged to the school and had to be kept in pristine condition. This was one of the many reasons Aaron gave for not wanting to practice.

Aaron's lessons continued through the school music program. His lessons at home continued for a while too, but he eventually lost interest … and then he lost the mouthpiece. We had to order a new one, and it took weeks to arrive. We then tried the piano. Aaron and I took lessons together. We had our fingers rapped for not curving them correctly, and both of us quit at the same time. Today, he plays the guitar and sings quite well — so the gift was always there, it just took a while to awaken it!

A little artistic licence here. I don't think I ever showed a fish tank in the house before this sketch, and I didn't show one later — unless it was in the clinic. It simply appeared for this gag. Later on, I paid more attention to such details, but at this time, I just drew whatever came to mind!

I had fun drawing this character. I had meant her to be very sexy and very nice — someone who would possibly come between Elly and John. She would make Elly jealous, in any case. As the library job continued, Susan became less and less visible. I couldn't quite resolve her relationship to the rest of the characters ... and, perhaps, I was afraid that life might imitate art!

I have always been interested in bugs and snakes and creepy-crawly things. The only thing I don't like to catch and examine in my hands are spiders, but they fascinate me just the same. When I was a kid, some of my insect "pets" succumbed to my examinations, and I would create small but elaborate burial ceremonies for them. When one of my garter snakes died, I buried him in a long, flat tie box and gift wrapped him before I put him into the ground. It was the least I could do.

I love yard sales.

This series of strips was done as we led up to our exodus from the north by going through everything we had accumulated in the six years we had lived there.

WHAT ARE YOU DOING IN THE CRAWL SPACE, MOM?

LOOKING FOR STUFF TO SELL AT THE YARD SALE.

YOU CAN'T SELL THIS! IT'S MY VERY FAVORITE THING IN THE WHOLE WORLD!!

WHAT IS IT?

THIS IS ALL THE STUFF I'VE COLLECTED THAT WE NEVER USE.

ELLY—THAT'S MY DUFFEL COAT! YOU CAN'T SELL MY DUFFEL COAT!

I HAVEN'T WORN IT BECAUSE I'M WAITING FOR THE STYLE TO COME BACK!

JOHN ... YOU WON'T **LIVE** THAT LONG!!!

The big treasure trove was in my mother-in-law's attic. She had meticulously saved everything. There were ancient skis and snowshoes, lampshades, and blinds. There were picture frames, bottles, quilt frames, and toys. There was a trunk filled with clothing — some of it her mother's. We found corsets, dresses, feathered hats, and knee-length knickers — some was moth-eaten, but most was like new.

WHY IS IT THAT WHEN I DECIDE TO SELL SOMETHING IT BECOMES TOO PRECIOUS TO PART WITH?

WE HAVE LOADS OF JUST PLAIN JUNK THAT NOBODY USES, WEARS OR PLAYS WITH!!

HEY! LET'S CHUCK OUT THIS HIDEOUS WALL CLOCK!

ARE YOU KIDDING? MY **MOTHER** GAVE ME THAT!!!

It took days to sort through everything. Behind every stack of familiar flotsam was stuff we never knew she had. Parting with some of it was going to be hard. We had several family meetings to determine the fate of Ruth and Tom's collection.

HEY, MAN! WHAT'S HAPPENING?

MOM'S HAVIN' A YARD SALE.

THE PEOPLE SHE WORKS WITH HAVE ALL BROUGHT THEIR JUNK OVER TO OUR PLACE.

YEAH? WHEN ARE THEY GONNA START THE SALE?

I DUNNO.

THEY'RE STILL BUYING JUNK FROM EACH OTHER.

The great Johnston yard sale was an epic event. Everyone in Lynn Lake knew that Ruth had squirreled away some fine stuff and looked forward to seeing what would be up for grabs. Tables had to be borrowed from the church next door. It took us two days to price everything and set it out on display. As luck would have it, the event took place on the day of the high school graduation. Students in their best duds crowded around the tables, trying to score a deal ahead of the old guys.

OK, I'LL GIVE YOU THIS FOR $2. IF YOU TAKE THE SPOONS AS WELL ...

WHERE HAVE ALL THESE PEOPLE COME FROM? SOME I'VE NEVER SEEN IN MY LIFE!

EASTGATE LIBRARY YARD SALE

I GO EFF'RY YARD SALE IN CITY—AN' I GIFF YOU THE 6 OUTA 10 FOR DIS VON.

NO REFRESHMENTS.

The town's mine was closing, and many people where forced to move. Despite the fact that we were all trying to downsize, Ruth had a fantastic turnout — her sale was like Christmas and Halloween and everyone's birthday rolled into one. If you didn't want or need a thing, you had to be there — it wasn't just a sale, it was an event! In typical Ruth fashion, she provided an assortment of homemade goodies — she was a great hostess. In the end, her hard work paid off!

WE'RE RUNNING OUT OF STUFF, ELLY, AND THE SALE DOESN'T END FOR ANOTHER HOUR!

EASTGATE LIBRARY YARD SALE

WAIT! I'LL RUN INTO THE HOUSE AND FIND SOME MORE JUNK!

WHAT DO YOU MEAN— TAKE OFF THESE PANTS?!!!

When the stock began to run low, we ran home and dug through our own stuff — even though we had already sold everything we wanted to get rid of. Ruth and Tom went back into their house and did the same.

ONE HALF HOUR TO GO — WE ARE SLASHING OUR PRICES, EVERYBODY!

EVERYTHING 50% OFF — DON'T MISS THESE BARGAINS!

YARD SALE

¡WHEW! THAT'S IT! WE DID IT. WE SOLD NEARLY THE WHOLE WORKS!

MOM?.....HAS ANYONE SEEN MY BICYCLE?

When the dust cleared we did discover a few things gone that we wanted to keep — and one item had been stolen. Not bad for a day of chaos!

SO NOW THAT THE CRAZINESS IS OVER, YOU CAN COUNT YOUR PENNIES.

PENNIES? JOHN, WE MADE OVER $800 ON THAT YARD SALE!

SOME IDIOT EVEN PAID $25 FOR OUR OLD BLACK AND WHITE TV!

.....I THOUGHT IT LOOKED FAMILIAR.

I forget exactly how much they made, but the image of Tom, the family accountant, tallying up the take will stay forever. He meticulously stacked and sorted every coin, smoothed and organized every bill, and is the only person I have seen (other than the senior vendors in Vancouver's China Town) use an abacus!

WELL, YOU CERTAINLY CLEARED OUT THE HOUSE, EL!

GETTING RID OF ALL OUR JUNK HAS GIVEN US A LOT MORE STORAGE SPACE!

WHAT ARE WE GOING TO DO WITH ALL THIS ROOM?

FILL IT WITH MORE JUNK!

My mom was a British cook — this meant we had well-cooked meats and boiled veggies. Spuds were a staple, and we could always count on her gravy … but her specialty was dessert. We had little to spend on fancy cuts of meat or fresh stuff out of season, so we had canned peas, frozen carrots, liver, beef hearts, chicken neck soup, corned beef and cabbage, and other dishes that, when left on the plate for any length of time, had about as much appeal as compost on a hot day. But … the promise of a good dessert was enough to make us chow down just about anything.

Mom made the best pastry in the world. Her puddings were to die for. She made tapioca pudding and caramel cream, chocolate and vanilla and rum butter sauce — all of which were great on ice cream if poured straight from the saucepan. There was pineapple fluff, apple brown betty, treacle tart, and cakes. There were muffins and doughnuts, cinnamon whirls, cookies, and bread. She made stuff from scratch, rarely using her massive recipe collection. Ingredients and measurements she just knew. At a time when everyone was struggling to get by, we were fortunate. Using dessert as a bribe for eating the main course might have been the wrong thing to do, but it worked!

Ladies … is this not our best form of therapy? We need each other more than we need Lycra, hair dye, and creams!

NO WANNA GO TO PLAYCARE TODAY, MOM... DON'T FEEL WELL.

MY FROAT HURTS -AN' MY EAR HURTS.

YOU CAN'T GET SICK THIS MORNING, ELIZABETH!

I'VE GOT TO GO TO WORK!

I'M ALL READY TO GO OUT- AND ELIZABETH IS SICK!!

NOW I HAVE TO CALL PLAYCARE, CALL THE LIBRARY, CHANGE MY PLANS...

WHEN I WASN'T WORKING, IT WAS NO PROBLEM IF YOU KIDS WERE SICK....

YEAH... YOU WERE A REAL MOM THEN!

Earlier in my career, when Aaron went to daycare and I worked outside the home, any time he was sick, it was miserable for both of us. First, I had to make sure he was too ill to go to daycare. I know it's irresponsible to send a kid out there to infect others, but I was a single mom who had to buy groceries, and a day off work meant a smaller paycheque. If I had to stay home with him, I felt guilty for resenting the time I missed at work — and mad at myself for feeling guilty.

...I GUESS I CAN DO THIS PROJECT AT HOME. IT'LL MEAN A FEW PHONE CALLS....

ELIZABETH-YOU'RE SICK! GET BACK INTO BED.

DON'T WANNA GO TO BED. WANNA BE WIF YOU!

HERE WE SEE THE TRUE MEANING OF THE WORDS- "WORKING MOTHER"!

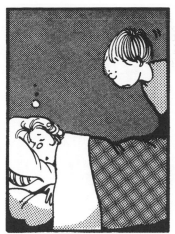

My brother and I fought a lot when we were kids, and Aaron and Kate did as well. When one kid is sick, however, the other's true colours bloom; any time Kate was ill, Aaron would be so concerned, I would almost have to keep him at home, too.

Neither Kate nor Aaron was ever so ill that they had to go to the hospital. We did live down the road, however, from a family whose young daughter had cystic fibrosis, and the threat of losing her was constant and cruel. Little Christine liked dolls, and I had a sizeable doll collection. I gave her one of my favourite handmade dolls, which started a sweet friendship. Visiting Christine and her family gave me new insight: It requires amazing strength of character to live with a chronic illness.

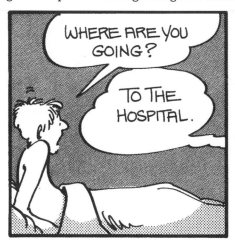

I think kids recover from illnesses well because they have such positive attitudes. When I was 18, I had my appendix out. Considering myself an adult, I was disappointed to be put in the children's ward. Surrounding me were kids recovering from all kinds of serious things, and all I could hear was laughter, music, and the sounds of the day. When I visited the adult ward, there were complaints, depression, subdued conversation, and an "old" smell. I was then glad to be where I was.

UNTIL WE GET SOME TESTS BACK, WE WON'T KNOW WHAT SHE HAS!

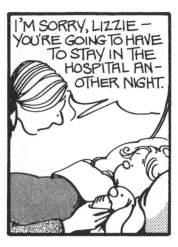

I'M SORRY, LIZZIE — YOU'RE GOING TO HAVE TO STAY IN THE HOSPITAL ANOTHER NIGHT.

ONE MORE NIGHT? HERE?

UH HUH.

IS THAT ALL?

DAD! SHE'S BACK! MOM'S BROUGHT LIZZIE HOME!

HOW IS SHE, ELLY? IS SHE ALL RIGHT?

CUT IT OUT! GIMME THAT! **MOM!** .... LIZZIE'S BUGGING ME!!

RIGHT BACK TO NORMAL!

SO — ELIZABETH'S OUT OF THE HOSPITAL AND FEELING FINE!

YEAH. IT ALL HAPPENED SO FAST. WE WERE SURE LUCKY. IT COULD HAVE BEEN A LOT MORE SERIOUS.

LIFE'S A FUNNY THING, STEVE .....

YOU NEVER KNOW WHAT'S AROUND THE CORNER!

This is such an old gag image, but I had to use it here. I actually showed Aaron how to squeeze our garden hose to stop the water flowing — so he could "surprise" someone. Naturally, I was his first surprisee!

111

Charles Schulz told me that this punch line was one of his favourites. "What a great line!" he said. "How do we think up these things?!!"

When I was about five, our road was tarred, and it took weeks for the surface to completely cure. Meanwhile, the tar bubbled out along the edges, and we kids played with it. I happen to love licorice, and when a friend (older and wiser — perhaps eight years old) told me that tar was liquorice, I believed him. I picked a ball of it off the road and chewed it. The taste was awful. I was told it would improve if I kept chewing, which I did. This proves, once again, that kids will believe anything!

Because I worked from home, there were moms in town who felt they could drop in for coffee any time. One of these ladies was very offended when I asked her to come when I wasn't working and to please call first. Both of her kids were in school; I was paying a sitter to watch Kate. Every hour at the drafting board meant time I could spend with my family later. It was a hard concept for some — who thought that doodling on paper couldn't possibly be work!

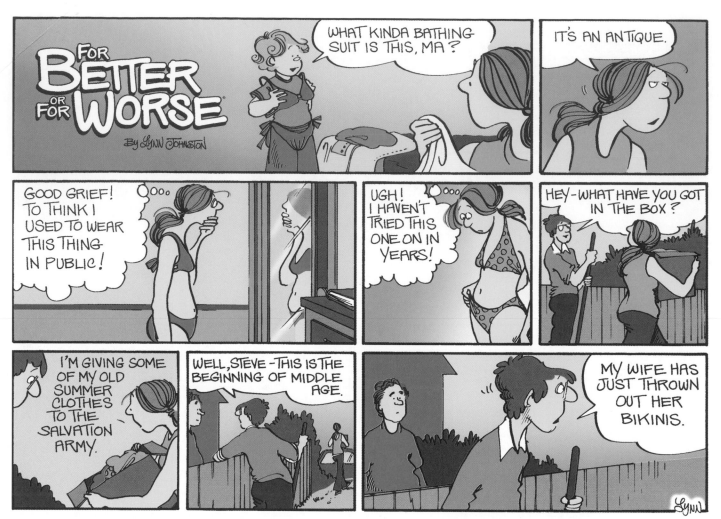

I have only owned one bikini in my life; I am one of those women on whom a bikini looks like "balloon art." After I turned 30, the bikini was no longer beachwear — it was beached-whale wear with stretch marks. Just trying it on in the bedroom was demoralizing. So now I go for the one-piece wonder — if I can find one that flatters. I'm still wearing the same suit I bought in Florida six years ago. Florida is the only place I've been where there is a reasonable choice in beachwear. In Canada, it is difficult to find a bathing suit in the winter … because who swims in January? Whoa! Millions of us escape the snow shovel for at least a week each winter, and with us, we take our spending money for summer duds. We HAVE to!

When it comes to purchasing a new bathing suit, I am not choosy; I will pay the price for a suit that has a flattering line, good frontal support, can be worn in public (even though I might never see these people again), does not have a bilious colour scheme, actually adheres to the body when wet, and doesn't let a cheek hang out if I stoop to retrieve a towel. This is the prize I look for as I peruse the shops in Florida. When I did this strip, it was not so much a slight toward my not so slightness but a loud complaint to those who design, manufacture, and present us with unwearable beachwear.

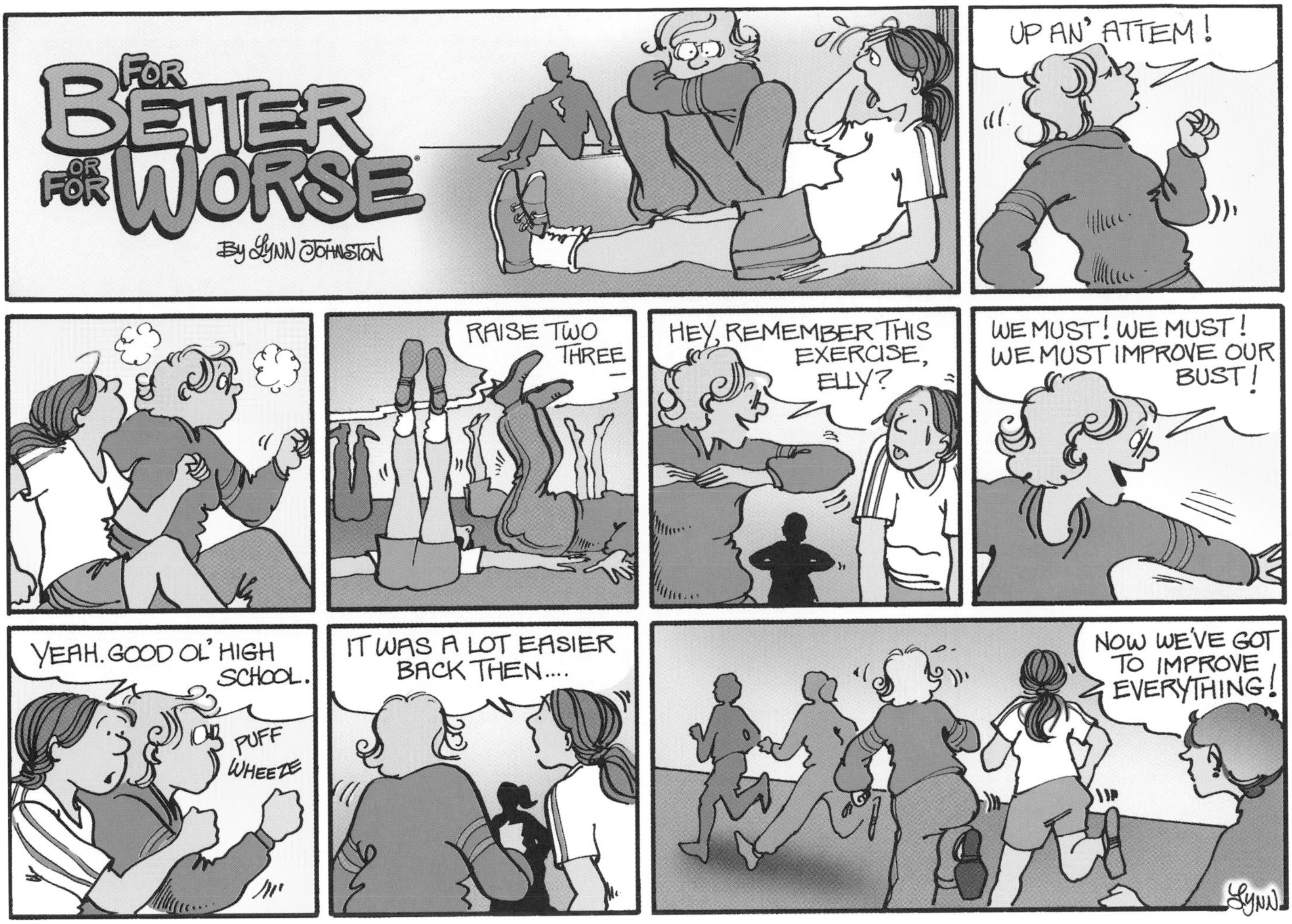
For Better or For Worse
By Lynn Johnston
UP AN' ATTEM!
RAISE TWO THREE
HEY, REMEMBER THIS EXERCISE, ELLY?
WE MUST! WE MUST! WE MUST IMPROVE OUR BUST!
YEAH. GOOD OL' HIGH SCHOOL.
PUFF
WHEEZE
IT WAS A LOT EASIER BACK THEN....
NOW WE'VE GOT TO IMPROVE EVERYTHING!
LYNN

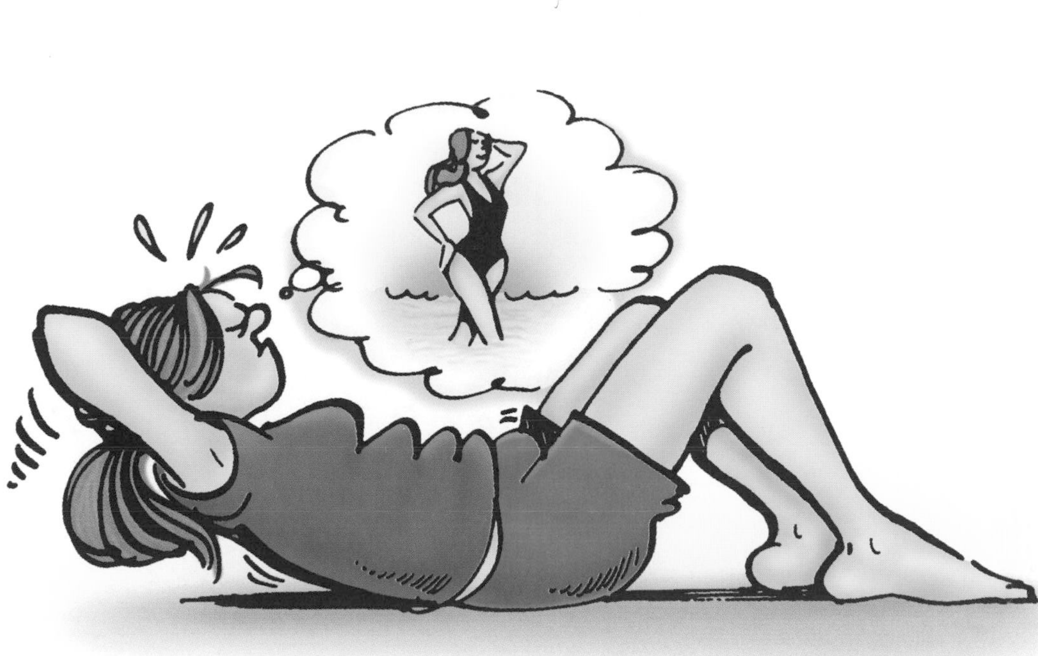

Like many dogs, Farley knew exactly what the word "bath" meant.

I had a good-sized washtub in the backyard. It would take two of us to get him to the tub and then into it. Once he was in, he gave up the fight and put up with the scrubbing.

After he was bathed and dried, it took another hour or more to comb out his fur and get him to look good again. The final touch was an elastic band in his hair to hold it away from his eyes. The ability to see, however, gave him a clear shot at the ravine behind our house or the nearest pile of stink he could roll in. I don't think he ever stayed clean for more than a day, but it was worth the effort just to have him smell good for a change!

Some of Aaron's friends did have keys to their houses, but again, the town was so small that we all looked out for each other. In general, the kids didn't get into too much trouble. Small towns are a relatively safe environment for kids — which is probably why all say they can't wait to leave when they hit their teen years!

Our old sofa had that soft, comfy look and feel that called out to you, "Take a naaaaapppp!" That sofa accepted you like a mother's arms, and once prone, you were there for as long as the family would allow. The springs were gone in the middle, the arms sagged, and the cushions were worn and discoloured. It exhaled the aromas of baby, breakfast, Scotchgard, and dust. It had been savaged and jumped on and badly treated — yet it was the most sought after roost in the house. My husband flopped down on it as soon as he came in from work, then Katie would flop on him. Aaron and his chums piled onto it to eat popcorn and watch television, and when it was my turn, I'd just curl up and fall asleep. When we left Lynn Lake, we left that couch behind. We bought a new one for the new house — it was a "Roxton." We also bought the chair and the end tables that went with it. This was a great-looking couch, and we had it for years … but it was never as nice as the old one. It never saw the rough and tumble of babies, the cushions were never turned into forts or pulled onto the floor for sleepovers, and nobody ever stood on the arms to put paper stars on the window for Christmas. There's something wonderful about an old couch. In its fabric and foam is a family's history — it held and supported each one of us through good times and bad!

We didn't own a car until I was about 10. Up until then, any road trips we went on were with my mother's parents in their '48 Ford. Our family would pile into the car, along with Grandma and Grandpa, and head out on an adventure. We would inevitably end up sitting in some old guy's living room, silently counting the stains on his wallpaper, while Gramps bought, sold, and traded stamps. These stops were deadly. With luck, if we behaved ourselves, we'd be rewarded with a picnic or a trip to the beach.

My grandfather was extremely strict, and being his car, we followed his rules. Alan and I would sit in the back of Gramp's car with a parent between us. If there was an argument, however, one of us would be moved to the front seat. My grandmother would get the window, which left me in the middle — within "cuffing reach" of Gramps. This was the "trouble spot," and I sat here often. From this spot, I had a clear view of the crackly old Blaupunkt radio on the underside of the dash. I can tell you today exactly what that radio looked like. It was ugly.

One day, Dad surprised us with a real Chevrolet. It was second-hand, two-toned green and white. We couldn't believe our eyes! We could now go anywhere we could afford to go — and our destinations were no longer determined by Gramps. Alan and I loved being able to open the back windows and let our hair blow in the wind. We didn't have to fight over a window because there was only the two of us in the back, but we did fight — we HAD to fight — it was something to do! These days, with all of the electronic goodies and gadgetry, kids are immersed in some form of entertainment from the beginning of a trip to the end, so perhaps backseat sibling feuds are fewer now. Perhaps.

My friends who were lucky enough to own a piano and get lessons often complained about the torture they suffered having to practice for recitals and such. Years later, with the stress of learning far behind them, they thanked their parents at long last for giving them the gift of music.

BEFORE YOU GO, I WANT TO FIND YOU SOME NICE TRAVELING CLOTHES.

WE DON'T WANT GRANDMA TO SEE YOU GETTING OFF THE PLANE LOOKING LIKE THAT!

YOU'LL BE A CLEAN AND TIDY YOUNG GENTLEMAN FOR A CHANGE.

THEN HOW'S SHE GONNA KNOW IT'S <u>ME</u>

When my mom suggested that Aaron go by himself to Vancouver for a visit, he was keen! This was a long journey, but he'd spent a lot of time in aircraft, was very independent, and had no fear at all of travelling alone. Besides, he knew he'd be spoiled rotten at the other end of his journey!

STAND UP STRAIGHT! PUT YOUR ARMS DOWN. STOP SCRATCHING!!

HOW AM I GOING TO SEE IF THESE FIT IF YOU DON'T STAND STILL!

ANYTHING I CAN DO TO HELP YOU IN THERE?

YES- HAVE YOU GOT ANYTHING IN A STRAIGHT-JACKET? SIZE 12?

This trip was quite an adventure for all of us. I preoccupied myself with organizing clothes and other things he had to take — which took my mind off losing him to the great world out there.

DO YOU REALLY THINK WE'RE DOING THE RIGHT THING — SENDING MICHAEL ON A PLANE ALL BY HIMSELF?

SURE. HE'S A BIG BOY. HE'LL BE ABLE TO HANDLE IT JUST FINE!

YEAH.

...BUT.... I DON'T THINK I WILL.

We questioned ourselves. Were we being too liberal? Too trusting? Was it wrong to let such a young boy go so far on his own?

Robert's Fine Jewellery was one of the flagship stores in Lynn Lake. It reminded me so much of my dad's store in North Vancouver that I had to include it in the strip. Having grown up surrounded by giftware, jewellery, and trinkets, I was never too interested in owning any of it, but after I left home and had my ears pierced, things changed. I started to really appreciate jewellery, and once in a while, even though I felt guilty for doing so, I'd buy myself something small, something nice.

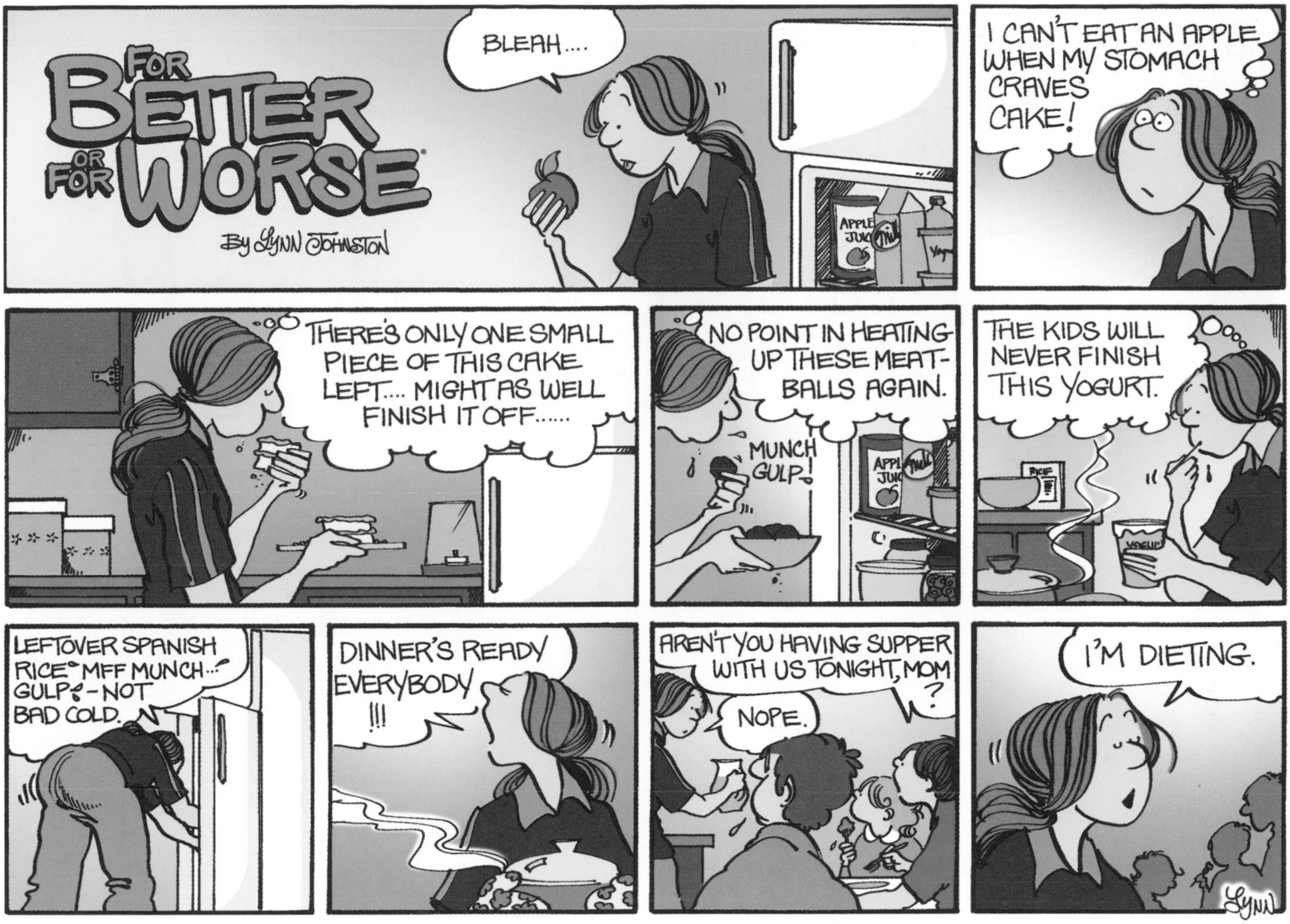
For Better or For Worse
By Lynn Johnston
BLEAH....
I CAN'T EAT AN APPLE WHEN MY STOMACH CRAVES CAKE!
THERE'S ONLY ONE SMALL PIECE OF THIS CAKE LEFT.... MIGHT AS WELL FINISH IT OFF......
NO POINT IN HEATING UP THESE MEAT-BALLS AGAIN.
MUNCH GULP!
THE KIDS WILL NEVER FINISH THIS YOGURT.
LEFTOVER SPANISH RICE - MFF MUNCH... GULP - NOT BAD COLD.
DINNER'S READY EVERYBODY !!!
AREN'T YOU HAVING SUPPER WITH US TONIGHT, MOM?
NOPE.
I'M DIETING.
Lynn

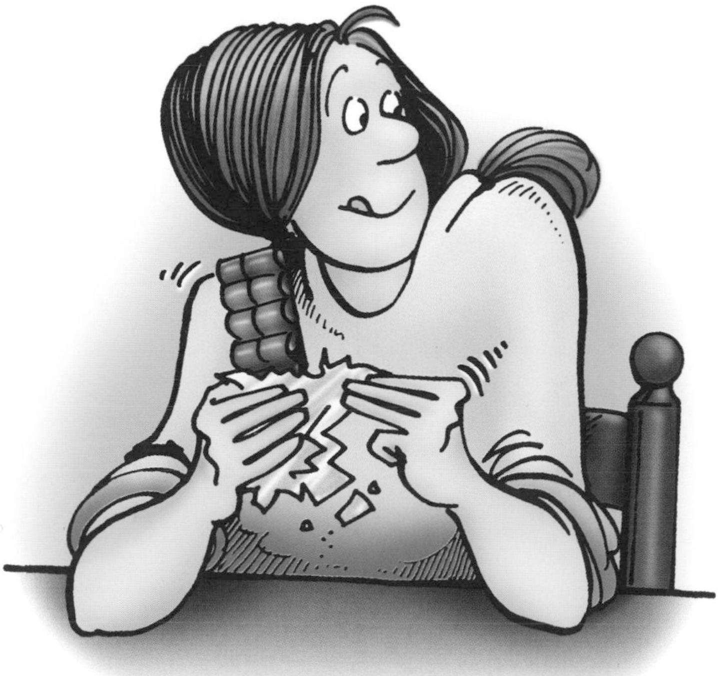

The thing Aaron liked about my brother's smoking was that he got to blow out the matches.

Alan might kill me for this, but as a little kid, he DID carry around a blanket. Actually, it was my blue chenille bedspread, which he inherited when the corners became twisted and grey. When it started to rot, Mom cut it up into smaller pieces so he'd have even more corners to chew on. By the time these pieces deteriorated, he was old enough to go to Beaver camp (junior Scouts in Canada), and Dad suggested he have a ceremonial blankie burning in the fireplace. Alan stuffed his remaining blankies into a shoebox. Dad put lighter fluid over the contents, made a hole in the lid, pulled out a wick of blankie, and the solemn ceremony took place. Al, with sadness and stoicism, sat and watched the box burn to ashes as Dad sat beside him with his arm around his shoulder. It was a coming of age for my brother and a time when Dad proved, beyond a doubt, that he understood kids better than anybody we knew!

Alan and me — early 1950s.

HMPH. ... DOESN'T LOOK CLEAN.

BLEAH! I DON'T WANT DIS PIECE OF CELERY - IT GOTS DIRT ON IT!

I WANNA NEW FORK, MOM - DIS ONE ISN'T WASHED RIGHT.

YUCK! DON'T WANT THE SOUP. IT TASTES FUNNY.

DON'T WANNA WEAR THE BLUE JACKET. IT GOTS APPLE JUICE DOWN THE FRONT!

GRUMBLE... SNARL...

ALL RIGHT, ELIZABETH. GO OUTSIDE, NOW AND PLAY!

126

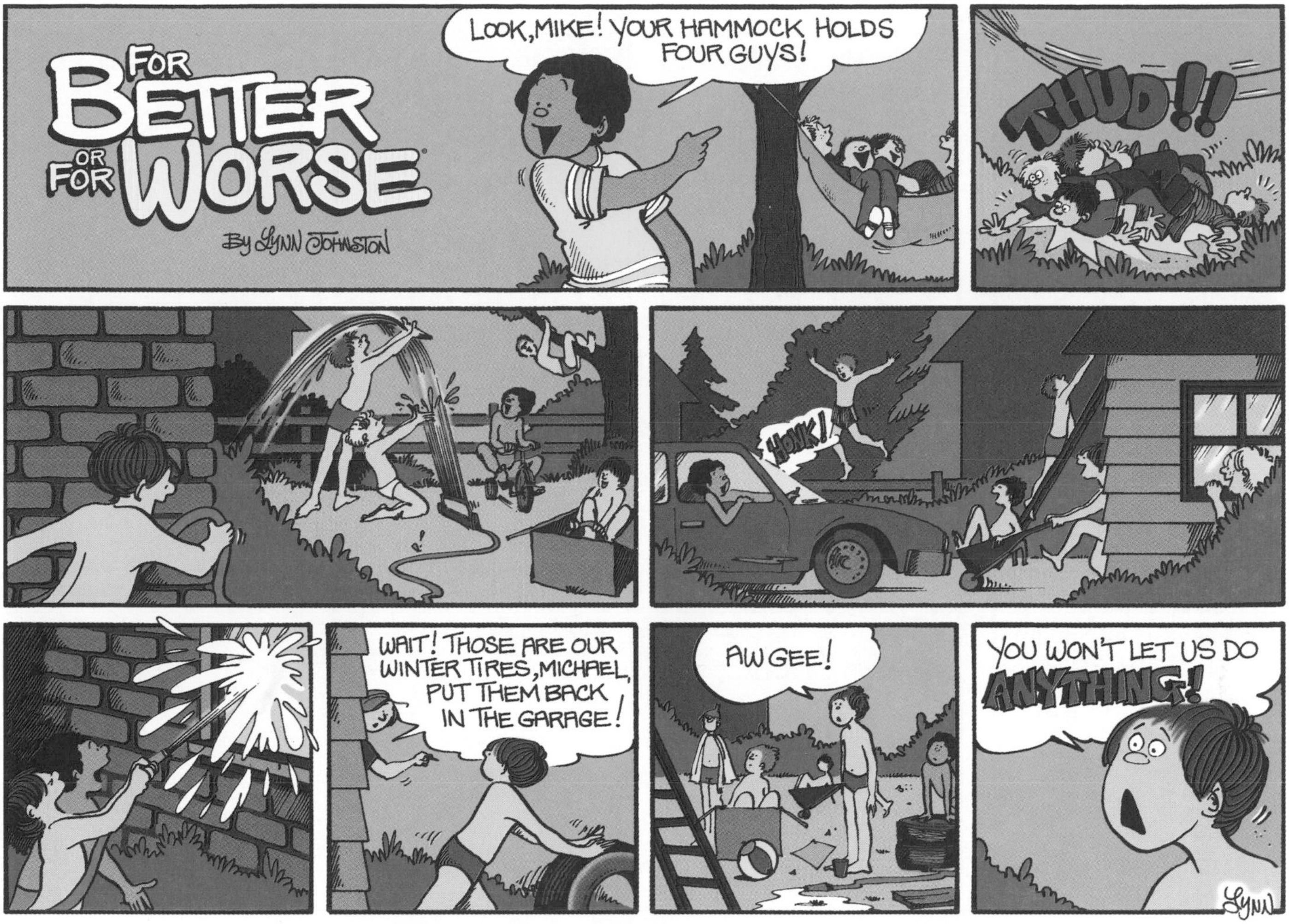
For Better or For Worse
By Lynn Johnston
LOOK, MIKE! YOUR HAMMOCK HOLDS FOUR GUYS!
THUD!!
HONK!
WAIT! THOSE ARE OUR WINTER TIRES, MICHAEL, PUT THEM BACK IN THE GARAGE!
AW GEE!
YOU WON'T LET US DO ANYTHING!
LYNN

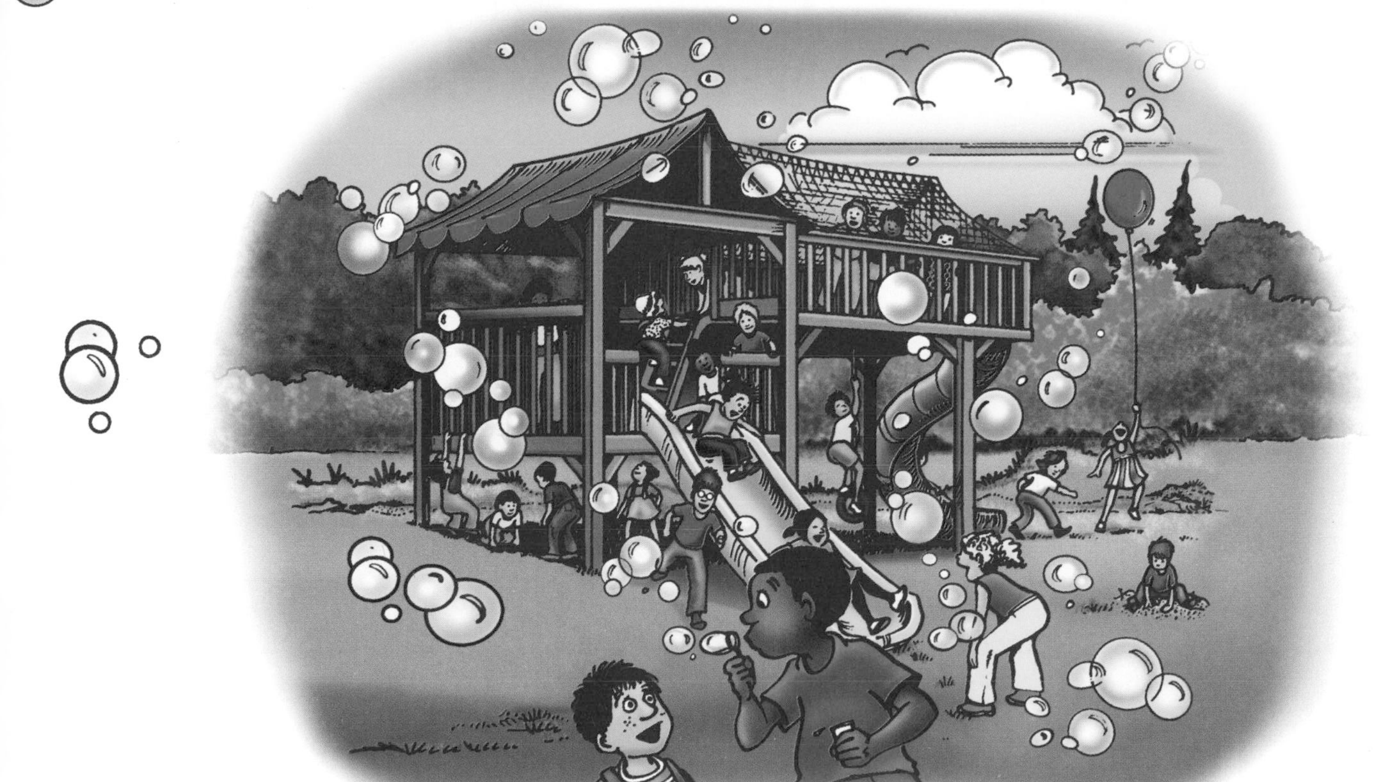

Aaron was eight years old when we decided to let him go to Vancouver by himself and visit my mom and dad. We were surprised by his courage. Most kids his age would have been terrified of flying alone — and for such a long distance.

I used this same punch line again years later, and even made it the title of a collection book. You'd think I'd remember every gag and not use it again, but sometimes I slipped up!

Yes, we did say it meant "untrained," but before he boarded the plane, we told him the truth!

STOP FIDGETING, ELLY! MICHAEL'S ON HIS WAY AND HE'LL BE JUST FINE.

HE'S GOT BOOKS, TOYS, — HE'LL GET PLENTY OF ATTENTION.

THERE'S NOTHING TO WORRY ABOUT.

CLICK!

FURTHER INVESTIGATION INTO THE FATAL CRASH OF A 737 PASSENGER JET HAS REVEALED THAT...

It was so hard to let Aaron get onto that plane alone. We worried about him all day. He had to change planes three times, and even though he was being monitored by friends and friendly airline staff, we couldn't sit still until he had safely arrived.

SURE IS PRETTY OUT THERE TODAY.

YEAH!

I KEEP LOOKING FOR ANGELS — BUT I HAVEN'T SEEN ANY.

DO YOU S'POSE IT'S THEIR DAY OFF?

IN PREPARATION FOR OUR DESCENT INTO CALGARY, PLEASE MAKE SURE YOUR SEATBELTS ARE....

YOUR SEATBELT, MICHAEL!

I CAN'T!

THERE WE ARE.

OOH!

IS THAT THE KID WHO ASKED FOR ALL THE LEFTOVER DESSERTS?

My mom called from the airport as soon as Aaron arrived in Vancouver. She said he was very sick. As it turned out, he'd noticed that many passengers did not eat their chocolate desserts and asked the hostess if he could have them all. Thinking he'd never eat ALL the desserts, they happily gave them to him and neglected to check back until he was too full to do up his seatbelt. He arrived in Vancouver engorged and miserable. My folks were too thoughtful to laugh — but we sure did!

YOUR MOM'S ON THE PHONE, EL. MICHAEL'S PLANE HAS BEEN DELAYED IN CALGARY!

MECHANICAL DIFFICULTY? TWO HOURS? ARE YOU SURE?

POOR MICHAEL! ALL BY HIMSELF AT A STRANGE AIRPORT!

WANT ANOTHER ROUND OF CARDS — OR SHOULD WE GO PLAY VIDEO GAMES?

SOMETHING'S WRONG WITH THE PLANE WE WERE ON, MIKE, SO WE'RE WAITING FOR ANOTHER ONE.

BOY. IT'S SURE TAKING FOREVER TO GET HERE!

SURE IS!

THIS MUST BE WHAT THEY MEAN BY JET-LAG."

WE'RE GOING, MIKE! GET YOUR STUFF! WE'RE GOING.

ARE YOU GONNA SIT WITH ME AGAIN?

WHEN I'M NOT WORKING — SURE, I'LL SIT WITH YOU.

TELL ME, KID—WHAT HAVE YOU GOT THAT I DON'T HAVE!

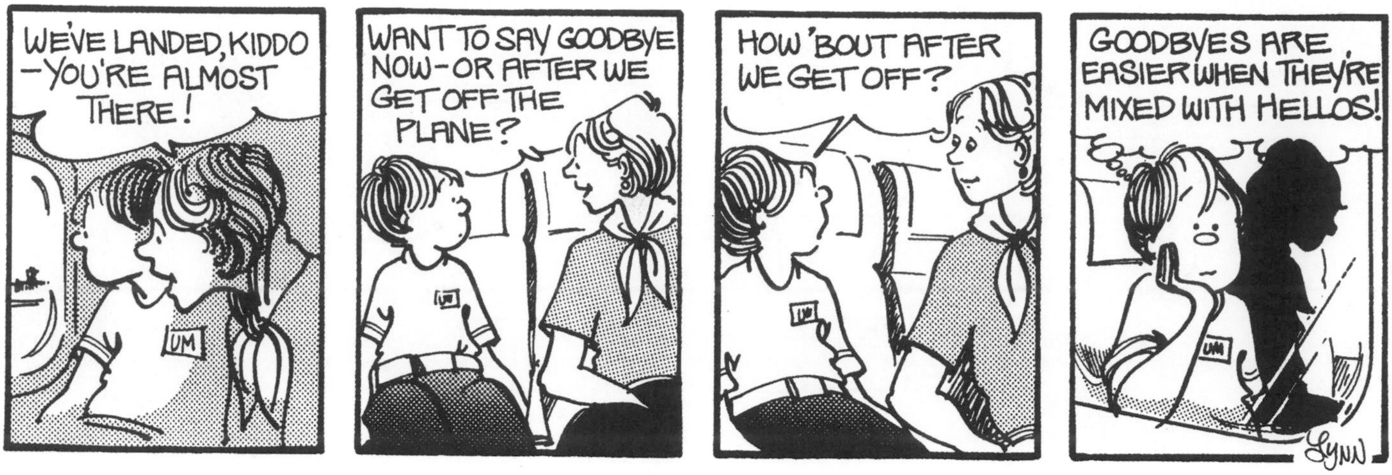
WE'VE LANDED, KIDDO -YOU'RE ALMOST THERE!
WANT TO SAY GOODBYE NOW-OR AFTER WE GET OFF THE PLANE?
HOW 'BOUT AFTER WE GET OFF?
GOODBYES ARE EASIER WHEN THEY'RE MIXED WITH HELLOS!
UM
LYNN

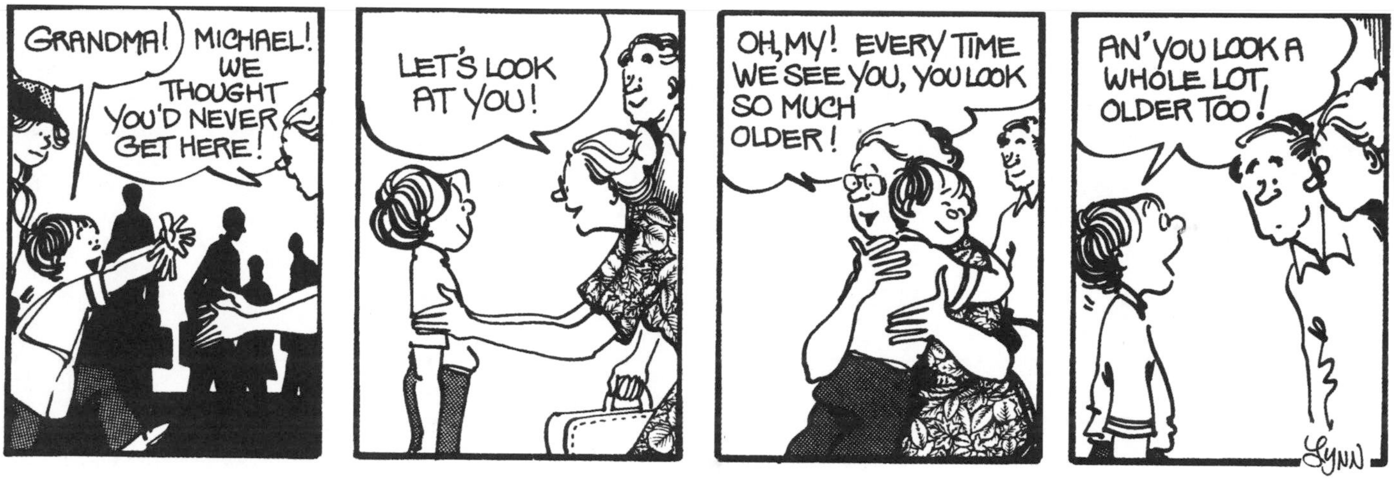
GRANDMA!
MICHAEL! WE THOUGHT YOU'D NEVER GET HERE!
LET'S LOOK AT YOU!
OH, MY! EVERY TIME WE SEE YOU, YOU LOOK SO MUCH OLDER!
AN' YOU LOOK A WHOLE LOT OLDER TOO!
LYNN

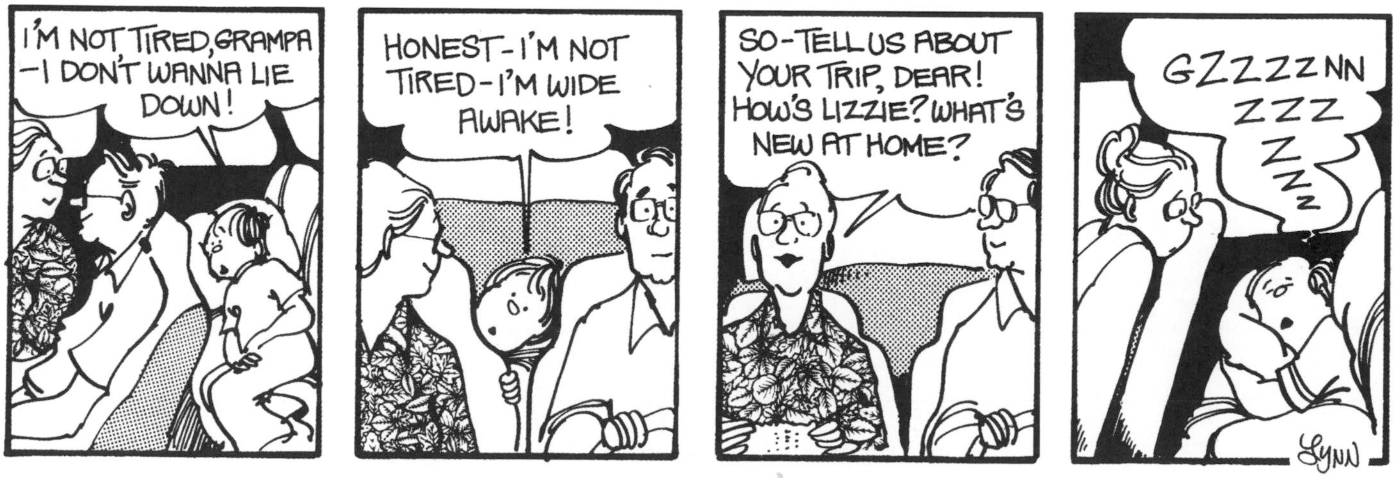
I'M NOT TIRED, GRAMPA -I DON'T WANNA LIE DOWN!
HONEST-I'M NOT TIRED-I'M WIDE AWAKE!
SO-TELL US ABOUT YOUR TRIP, DEAR! HOW'S LIZZIE? WHAT'S NEW AT HOME?
GZZZZNN
ZZZ
ZZZ
LYNN

Aaron had a wonderful time in Vancouver. He was spoiled and pampered, and if he ever felt that he was getting less attention than his little sister, he was well compensated by the way my folks doted on him. Ahhh, this is what grandparents are for!

When this strip appeared, I had immediate responses from stargazers who told me that on that date in our time zone, the crescent would be going in the other direction. They were right. From this time on, I made sure I checked out the phases of the moon on our calendar before drawing a moon in the sky!

My father loved to dance. He would pick me up and dance with me until I fell asleep in his arms. He could sing so well and knew the words to so many songs that he never seemed to run out of waltzes or shanties or tunes from the bar. I remember the swoop of his body as he waltzed to the "Blue Danube" with theatrical panache. He could two-step and tango and polka and jive, and I melted into his shoulder with the rhythm and the warmth of his style.

Last November, my daughter, Katie, and her husband, Lane, presented me with my first grandchild. Laura is now almost one year old, and she loves to dance with me. I hold her the way my father held me. I sing the same songs, and I move with the same style. I thank him again and again for this memory and a gift that I'm now passing on.

135

RIGHT AROUND THIS POINT HERE IS MY OWN SECRET FISHING HOLE, MIKE!

I'VE NEVER TOLD AN-OTHER SOUL... SO JUST YOU AN' I KNOW ABOUT IT!

LOOK, GRAMPA, THERE'S ALREADY 3 OTHER BOATS IN THERE!

DARN! WE WERE FOLLOWED!!

DID YOU TAKE MOM AN' UNCLE PHIL FISHING WHEN THEY WERE LITTLE?

OH, SURE. BUT I DIDN'T HAVE MUCH TIME THEN. NOT MUCH MONEY, EITHER.

...NOW I'VE GOT ME A BOAT AND PLENTY OF TIME... BUT ELLY AND PHIL ARE GROWN AND GONE.

LIFE SOMETIMES WORKS BACKWARD..... DOESN'T IT, GRAMPA.

YESSIR-I CAN SEE THESE BABIES NOW... FRIED IN BUTTER—JUST WAITING FOR US TO SINK OUR TEETH INTO 'EM!

YEAH! I WONDER WHAT GRANDMA WILL SAY WHEN SHE SEES THEM!

YOU CAUGHT 'EM-YOU CLEAN 'EM!!

ON SECOND THOUGHT... THEY'D BE GOOD FOR THE GARDEN.

The fish Aaron caught with my dad were not great eating, and Aaron was very disappointed when Mom dug them into the garden. For the next fishing trip, Mom and Dad were prepared. When the men came home with fish for the table, Aaron believed he was chowing down on his catch. Sometimes a white lie comes in the form of frozen fillets.

SEE? CLEANING A FISH IS NO PROBLEM.
SLIT 'ER OPEN, EMPTY 'ER OUT... CHOP 'ER HERE, SCALE 'ER LIKE THIS...
THERE! ALL READY TO FRY! WHAT DO YOU SAY, MIKE?
COULD I HAVE A HOT DOG?
LYNN

I'M FINE, MOM, I'M HAVING A GREAT TIME!

WE WENT FISHING, WE WENT TO THE ZOO AN' THE BEACH AN' THE WATER SLIDES...

...GRANDMA AN'I ARE GOING TO THE PLANE-TARIUM TOMORROW— AN' THEN WE'RE GOING OUT TO DINNER...

CAN I STAY HERE FOREVER?!!

THERE, THAT'S A GOOD JOB WELL DONE!

WITH MICHAEL AWAY, I'VE BEEN ABLE TO CLEAN OUT HIS ENTIRE ROOM!

HE'LL NEVER MISS ALL THE JUNK I'VE THROWN OUT. BESIDES.... WHO'S GOING TO TELL HIM?

WHEN'S MICHAEL COMING HOME?

IN A FEW DAYS.

WHEN? HUH? WHEN'S HE COMING HOME?

SOON!

WHY DO YOU KEEP ASKING THE SAME QUESTION, ELIZABETH!?

...CAUSE IT ISN'T THE SAME WIFOUT HIM.

Even though she was the centre of attention when he was gone and even though they fought often, Katie really missed her older brother. She'd lie awake and talk about him. One night, she even asked if she could sleep in his bed.

138

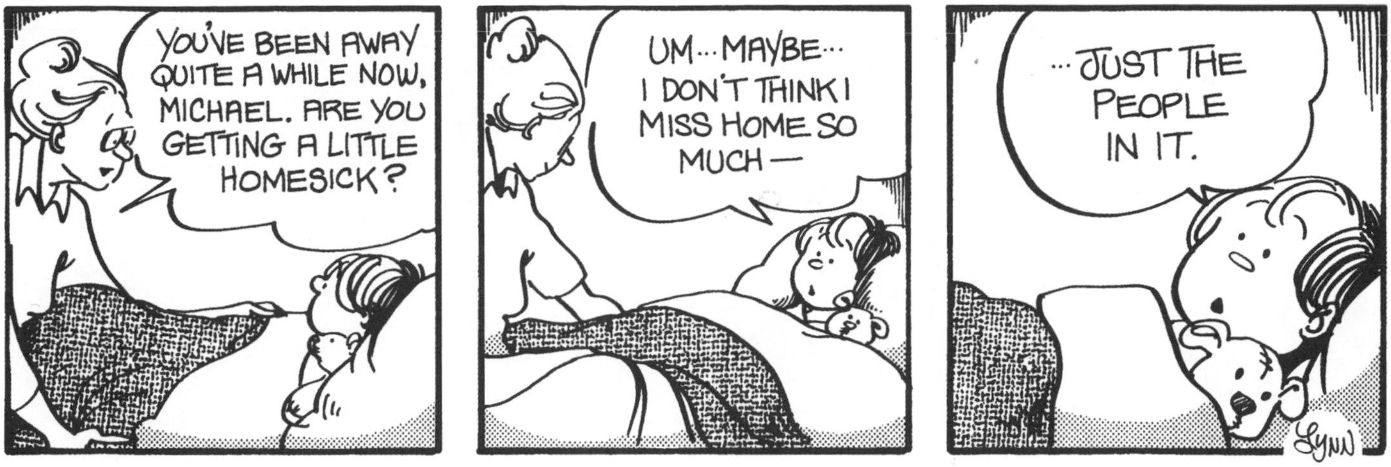
YOU'VE BEEN AWAY QUITE A WHILE NOW, MICHAEL. ARE YOU GETTING A LITTLE HOMESICK?
UM... MAYBE... I DON'T THINK I MISS HOME SO MUCH —
...JUST THE PEOPLE IN IT.
LYNN

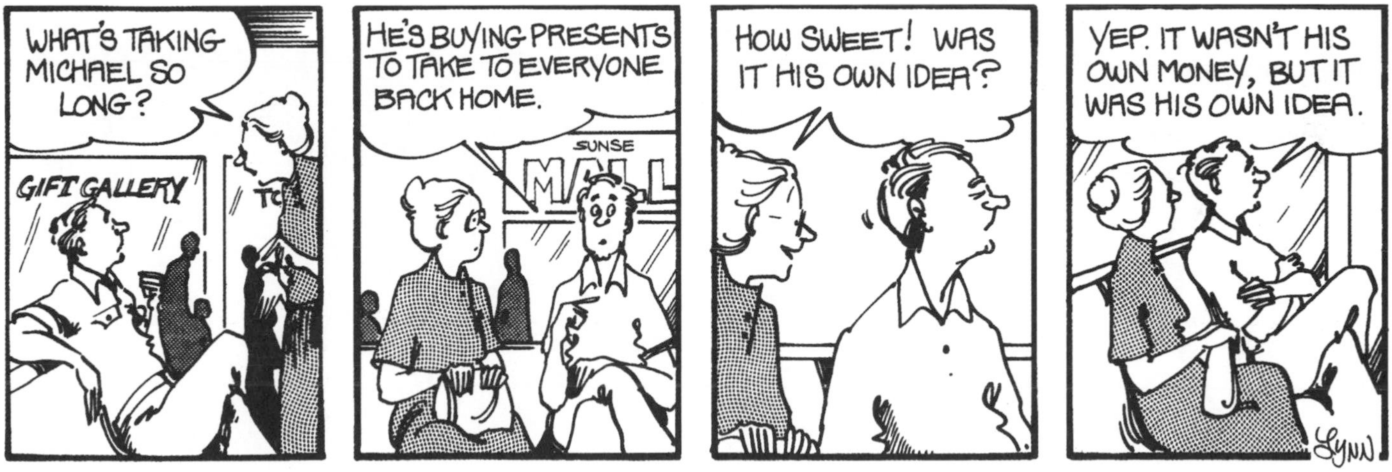
WHAT'S TAKING MICHAEL SO LONG?
GIFT GALLERY
HE'S BUYING PRESENTS TO TAKE TO EVERYONE BACK HOME.
HOW SWEET! WAS IT HIS OWN IDEA?
YEP. IT WASN'T HIS OWN MONEY, BUT IT WAS HIS OWN IDEA.
LYNN

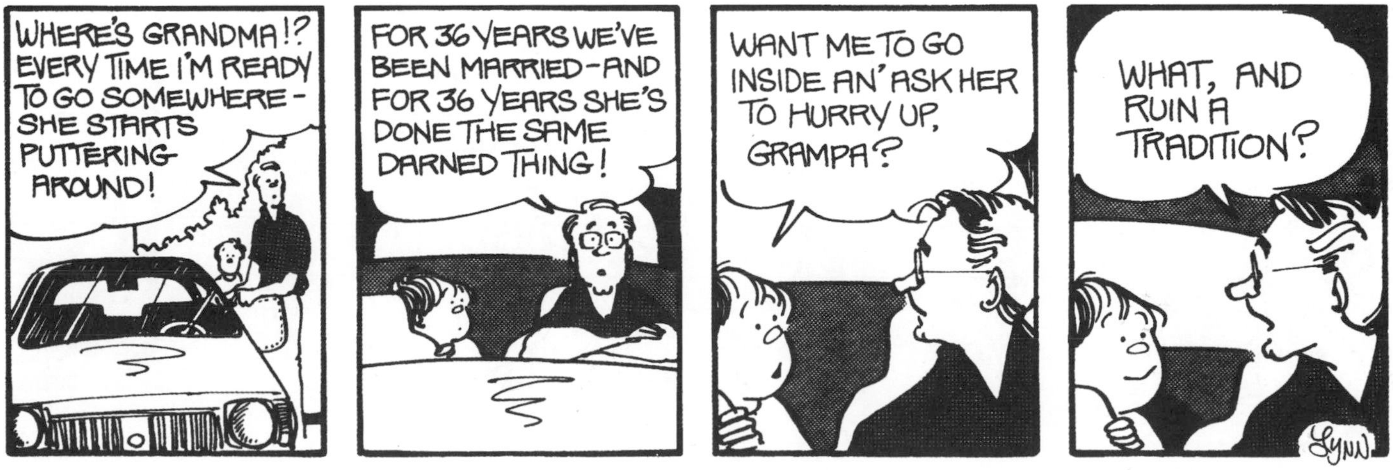
WHERE'S GRANDMA!? EVERY TIME I'M READY TO GO SOMEWHERE - SHE STARTS PUTTERING AROUND!
FOR 36 YEARS WE'VE BEEN MARRIED - AND FOR 36 YEARS SHE'S DONE THE SAME DARNED THING!
WANT ME TO GO INSIDE AN' ASK HER TO HURRY UP, GRAMPA?
WHAT, AND RUIN A TRADITION?
LYNN

This really happened — Katie did hide in a photo booth. Unfortunately, we were too upset to have her picture taken!

ANYONE SEEING A LITTLE GIRL AGE 4, WEARING A YELLOW T-SHIRT...

LAST SEEN ON ARRIVALS FLOOR ...ANSWERING TO THE NAME OF ELIZABETH PATTERSON...

PHOTOS 50¢

LISTEN, BUNNY—SOMEONE HERE GOTS THE SAME NAME AS ME!!

Lynn

AIR CANADA FLIGHT 119 FROM VANCOUVER IS NOW ARRIVING AT GATE—

AAAGH! THAT'S MY SON'S PLANE—AND ELIZABETH IS STILL MISSING!

GO MEET YOUR PLANE, MA'AM, WE'LL FIND HER —DON'T WORRY.

SECURITY

I'M NOT WORRIED... I'M **HYSTERICAL!**

Lynn

MOM? MOM! WHERE'S MOM?!

WHAT'S THE MATTER, DEAR? WHERE'S YOUR MOMMY?

I DUNNO!!

I WEN' IN DERE TO SIT DOWN... AN' WHEN I CAME OUT—

SHE WAS **LOST!**

Lynn

Aaron did bring a gift for each one of us — fortunately, there were no crabs. This idea came from one of my own attempts to keep wildlife. Trips to the beach on the west coast often included digging in the tide pools, where we'd find all kinds of neat sea creatures. One day I brought home a pail full of crabs, which I left in the trunk of the car. I didn't remember them until my mom said there was a horrible smell coming from the trunk. That smell stayed for weeks … and so did Mom's anger!

This photo of Aaron is a favourite.

LICK! SLURP-LICK

OOH! UGH!

CUT IT OUT, FARLEY- STOP LICKING ME!

YOU'VE BEEN AWAY SO LONG- HE'S JUST HAPPY TO SEE YOU!

YEAH! MAYBE HE FORGOTS WHAT FLAVOR YOU ARE!

MOM THREW OUT YOUR OL' BATMAN CAPE WHILE YOU WERE GONE, MICHAEL.

SHE THREW OUT A RED CAR, A PAINT SET, SOME CHALK, SOME COMICS, LOTSA PAPER...

AAAGH!!! NOT MY PAINTS! NOT MY CAPE! LEMME SEE!

MOM WAS WRONG! SHE SAID HE'D NEVER NOTICE!

TOY CHEST

THE THINGS I THREW OUT OF YOUR ROOM WERE BROKEN, RUSTY AND OLD, MICHAEL.

BUT THEY WERE MINE! YOU CAN'T THROW OUT MY STUFF WITHOUT ASKING ME FIRST!

AND I SAY IF YOU REALLY WANTED THOSE THINGS, YOU'D HAVE LOOKED AFTER THEM IN THE FIRST PLACE!

I DID LOOK AFTER THEM! I KEPT THEM, DIDN'T I?

He was right to be angry, and I did apologize. I should have known better — after all, this is something my mom once did to me!

WHAT'S GOING ON HERE? MICHAEL'S ONLY JUST COME HOME AND THERE'S TROUBLE ALREADY!

WE'RE A FAMILY AGAIN! WE LOVE EACH OTHER!

NOW—WHAT'S THE POINT IN CONTINUING THIS ARGUMENT?

I WAS WINNING!!

MICHAEL, YOU'RE FILTHY! WHERE HAVE YOU BEEN!?

GORDON'S DAD TOOK US TO THE DUMP TO SEE IF WE COULD FIND MY STUFF YOU THREW OUT.

WE LOOKED ALL OVER. BUT WE COULDN'T FIND IT.

SO I BROUGHT HOME SOMEBODY ELSE'S STUFF INSTEAD!

CAN YOU BELIEVE IT? SOMEBODY ACTUALLY THREW OUT THIS PLASTIC BASEBALL BAT!

IT'S SPLIT DOWN THE SIDE. YOU COULD FILL IT FULL OF JUNK AN' SWING IT AROUND!

THERE'S SO MUCH NEAT STUFF AT THE DUMP. I'D LOVE TO WORK THERE WHEN I GROW UP!

'COURSE—MOM'D WANT ME TO GO TO UNIVERSITY FIRST.

My husband had all kinds of models. He loved to make them just for the fun of figuring them out. He even built a model aircraft when we were on our honeymoon, so modelling was definitely in his blood. He could focus for hours, shaving off an infinitesimal piece of plastic here, fitting an impossibly tiny piece there. He had endless patience when it came to building complicated model ships, vehicles, and aircraft. Interestingly, he had much less patience with kids!

Rod spent every minute he could in his treasured workshop. He could make or repair almost anything. Even though he was usually very careful, there were times when he did go to the clinic with a bandage or two! This always gave his patients a laugh and inspired me to do this strip.

The quote "my lungs sound like a barn full of owls" came from my dad. He was a pack-a-day smoker whose health was steadily deteriorating. Cigarettes were a staple for many musicians, but Dad's declining health and Alan's growing maturity made him see that he had to quit before he couldn't play the trumpet any more.

We all experienced the pain of withdrawal with him.

When he found himself checking the garbage for butts, he realized what a serious addiction smoking was!

This was an actual quote from my brother. I whooped when he said it. Not only was it funny, it was a punch line I didn't have to come up with!

149

Now that I am dogless, I find dog breath hard to take. When I had Farley, his breath came with warm licks, and his enquiring sniffs were more than welcome. Even so, there were times when I couldn't stomach the smell. Once, when Farley ate my chives, I was overwhelmed by his breath, but there was one time that was much worse; I was standing at my kitchen window watching him happily lying on the warm driveway, chewing something he'd found with obvious relish. He chewed with that look of ecstasy, the look children have when they're eating ice cream, that blissful satisfaction that comes with flavour and fun and mouth-watering fulfillment. He'd toss his head back, reposition his prize, and chew again. He was happy. Eventually, my curiosity got to me and I went out to see what succulent something he was chewing on. I couldn't believe my eyes. The object he was blissfully savouring was a flat, well-rotted, dried-out toad. To Farley, it was dog jerky. To me, it was horrible. I would have shown the true source of Farley's halitosis, but really, it was too gross for publication!

So many times I ran around my neighbourhood with a finger or a plastic gun, pointing at friends and crying, "BANG! You're dead!" It was exciting. It was fun. We heard the headline news and listened to our parents. Dad had been in the war, but nothing they said made a difference. We were on a mission to win something. We didn't know what. There was no real sense to it, nobody explained why we were fighting or what death meant. We were just caught up in the thrill and the energy and the noise and the fun. Later, as a cartoonist, I saw a striking similarity to a child's attitude and what really happens in a war.

I remember being so bored, I thought the day would never end. I'd lie on our old blue sofa and wish I could see into the future so I could know what to prepare for. I wanted to get started as soon as possible. Art came so easily for me (I never expected it to provide a living), so I worried about not being smart enough, not being liked, and not fitting in. Being a kid had so many limitations. I wanted to be grown up and gone! I felt imprisoned in a kid's body.

I have always been at least ten pounds over the weight I want to be. When my brother was in the agonizing throes of nicotine withdrawal, I likened it to not being able to have a second helping of spuds and gravy, and he said it was not the same. I argued. I thought it was exactly the same. He just had to practice a little self-denial. He said I was completely out to lunch. Having never been a smoker, I really had no idea what he was going through.

The first day of school was always exciting for me, and a new teacher was fresh meat. The ones who were most successful in taming our classes began by setting down the rules. They were strict, no-nonsense people who could stand up to the most irritating kids. If they also turned out to be creative, entertaining, funny, and fair, they had us in the palms of their hands, and we learned — just to earn their praise.

When I read that saying "I don't do mornings," I see someone who doesn't have kids. If you have a family, you do mornings until everyone is grown and gone. You do mornings in your pyjamas and housecoat, and if you're lucky, you can swill down a coffee while you dress. The only family member with the luxury of NOT doing mornings is the family pet, who simply wonders why everything has to be so complicated.

Alan bought and tried a cigarette substitute. It was a plastic inhaler with a nicotine hit. He wandered about the house trying to look nonchalant while sucking on an adult pacifier, but like all the other "quit the habit" innovations, this too was destined for failure. I had to give him credit — at least he tried. And when he flung the bogus butt into the woods one day, he didn't swear in front of the kids.

In parenting magazines, I read about "you messages." This is when someone turns a situation around and puts the pressure on YOU. We were taught that "you messages" were not good disciplinary tools and should not be employed when having a heart-to-heart conversation. Rather than say, "You made me angry today," a parent should say, "I felt angry today, and we need to talk." I practiced this as much as possible, but the art of defusing a situation by not putting guilt onto the other person failed to precipitate down to the offspring. Things that I could not possibly be responsible for suddenly became my fault. This candy wrapper incident enlightened me to the fact that my kids were as good at game playing with words as we were!

Leaving Lynn Lake saddens cartoonist

By Bradley Bird

Lynn Johnston says she's heartbroken about leaving Lynn Lake, but the town's declining economy simply drove her and her family away.

"We had no future in Lynn Lake," says Johnston, the 37-year-old creator of the comic strip, For Better Or For Worse. "It was very hard to feel at home there. You can't invest in a town like that."

Johnston, husband Rod and children Katie, 6, and Aaron, 11, moved from the northern Manitoba mining town to North Bay, Ont., in June.

Lynn Lake, population 1,800, has lost 1,700 people since 1972, largely because of layoffs. Its only working mine is set to close next year, and that would mean the loss of 300 more jobs. Town officials fear the closing would cut tax revenues so much that water and sewer services would be in jeopardy.

"It's kind of a heartbreaking thing," the cartoonist says about the move from Lynn Lake. "When you move away, you realize how wonderful a place it was."

Seemed tired

After spending a day signing dozens of autographs, Johnston, in Winnipeg to talk about two new compilations of her work, *Just One More Hug* and *Our Sunday Best*, seemed tired and harried — much as Elly Patterson often appears in her comic.

For Better Or For Worse appears in more than 600 newpapers in 11 countries and six languages. Johnston commands a six-figure salary but declined to say exactly how much she earns.

She and her husband bought 127 acres near North Bay because the property is near her hometown of Collingwood and closer to major Ontario cities though still secluded.

Most of the property is forested but some of it is meadow, Johnston says. They're living in a two-storey log house.

"It's the sort of thing Rod has been wanting to do. And I've been wanting a log house." It's a place where she can escape from publicity and relax with family and friends, one of the simple pleasures she enjoys. Her in-laws also live on the property.

She says she didn't move to the United States because, as a Canadian, she didn't want to, and she didn't move to a large city because she prefers the privacy of smaller centres. North Bay has a population of 50,567 and is about 330 kilometres north of Toronto on Lake Nipissing.

Respite for Phil

We won't be seeing much of comic character Phil for a while, Johnston says.

"I'm laying off Phil a little bit because my brother really does exist."

He's a school teacher near Ottawa and he took exception to some of her portrayals of him as a boozer, a smoker and a womanizer.

His students teased him about the way he was shown in the strips so he phoned to say, "Sis, it's time to lay off Uncle Phil. I'm suffering."

But Phil has a great sense of humor, and some her funniest lines have come from him. Once at home when he was fiddling with his hands and trying to quit smoking, Johnston suggested he eat a carrot, a healthy food.

"Healthy, you call this healthy?" he replied. "It's spent its entire life buried in dirt!"

Lynn Johnston: to Ontario

The article said I was heartbroken. I was to the extent that we were leaving some wonderful friends, but the town of Lynn Lake had seen much better days. People were finding work elsewhere, shops were closing, windows were being boarded up, and it was time to move on. Many people were setting their sights on Winnipeg, but we liked the north. We wanted to find a place that had the same small-town feel as Lynn Lake and yet had a thriving population. North Bay had been recommended by friends whose parents lived on nearby Trout Lake (where I happen to live, now.)

Bob and Patti suggested we fly over the lake and see how nice it is, but they warned us to avoid one peninsula because "a crazy lady, who is known to shoot at small aircraft, lives there." Intrigued, we flew over the property at 4,000 feet, figuring a rifle couldn't do much damage to us at this height. As it happened, the land was for sale, and we instantly fell in love with it.

Views of Trout Lake

THE RED BRICK HOUSE ON MACPHERSON DRIVE.

The view of Ruth and Tom's house from our mailbox.

Bob and Patti's friend Lena was a real estate agent who had, at one time, been a psychiatric nurse. Lena didn't think we needed an appointment to drive down the dirt road, which bordered the land, so we accompanied her down the lane, turned around, and came back. The sun was just going down. There in the glow of our headlights stood Thelma Haggard with her hands on her hips, blocking our exit. We'd been told she was a character. I thought she might be a sweet lady who was, perhaps, lonely and misunderstood, but Thelma was frightening! She was short, wide, and muscular. Her sparse hair had been dyed a dark red and was tightly wound around a few rows of old-fashioned metal rollers — the kind that fastened with an elastic and a small rubber ball. Her long green sweater was stretched over an immense and pendulous bosom, her bum-like cleavage smiling between the buttons. We stopped obediently. She approached the driver's side window like a cop. She pushed her head into the car and had a good look. Through green teeth, she hissed, "Nobody drives down here without me knowing who they are! You wanna get shot? How can I know you're not some kinda snakes comin' out here to get me?!" Lena tried to calm her down by explaining that we were interested in buying her property and had only driven down the lane (which was a public access) to have a look. Placated, Thelma agreed to meet us the next day. Without dickering over the price, we made an offer, which was accepted, and in no time the deed was done. As soon as we became the new owners, Thelma accused us of stealing her land and refused to move out of the house. "That's OK," we said, "don't move. We won't be leaving Lynn Lake right away, so just make sure the place is kept in good order — see that the pipes don't freeze." Thelma replied, "I'm not payin' no rent!!" "Fine," we said, "don't pay any rent, that's no problem." "In that case, I'm MOVIN'!" she shouted. And that was the end of it.

The following year, the neighbouring property came up for sale. On it was an unfinished log house. Rod always wanted to build a log house — another fine coincidence! So, without hesitation, we bought this house too.

THE NEW HOUSE IN CORBEIL

A sketch of the log house on our 1984 Christmas card.

As far as work was concerned, moving was a complicated venture. Before I could interrupt the production of a syndicated feature (by taking a holiday, moving, or even having surgery), I had to make sure that enough work had been sent to the syndicate to cover my absence. The rule of thumb was: send six weeks of dailies and eight weeks of Sunday pages past the expected date of my return. Before I even began to pack up, I worked weekends, evenings, and holidays in order to "bank" my material. We were all anxious and emotionally drained. Tearing ourselves away from friends and familiar surroundings was difficult, and working so hard compounded the stress. I remember just hanging in as we put our possessions into the moving van and loaded the kids and the rest of our stuff into the plane.

Fortunately, we had already made some friends in North Bay and were looking forward to living in the log house. Interestingly, the publisher of the *North Bay Nugget* had refused to put my strip into the local paper, but a writing campaign launched by some of the dentists and their families changed his mind. *For Better or For Worse* debuted in our new hometown around the same time we did! Ruth and Tom moved into Thelma's red brick house — just down the road, so once again, the grandparents were just a few minutes walk away. This was a blessing for all of us.

North Bay is located on one of the original voyageur routes. Fur traders entered the north by way of the Ottawa and Mattawa rivers. They portaged into Trout Lake, crossed the La Vase wetlands into Lake Nipissing, and travelled to the Great Lakes through the French River. It is a canoeist's paradise. Our community is also significant for being the birthplace of the Dionne Quintuplets. After years of neglect, the Dionne family home was moved from the small town of Callander to North Bay and is now a landmark and a monument to the five girls whose images are still recognized as the miracle that raised the morale of Canadians during the second world war. Unfortunately, the publicity destroyed a large and very private family in the process.

Now that we have lived in this historic and beautiful part of Ontario for over twenty-five years, we feel at home. We have many friends and lots of good memories. We're considered locals. ALMOST!

159

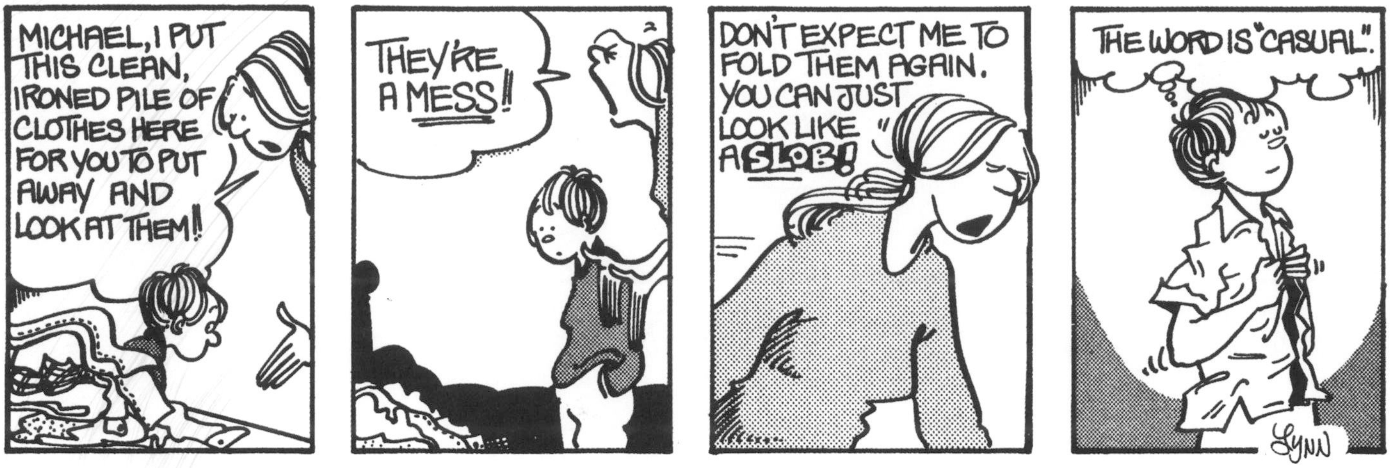
MICHAEL, I PUT THIS CLEAN, IRONED PILE OF CLOTHES HERE FOR YOU TO PUT AWAY AND LOOK AT THEM!!
THEY'RE A MESS!!
DON'T EXPECT ME TO FOLD THEM AGAIN. YOU CAN JUST LOOK LIKE A SLOB!!
THE WORD IS "CASUAL".
LYNN

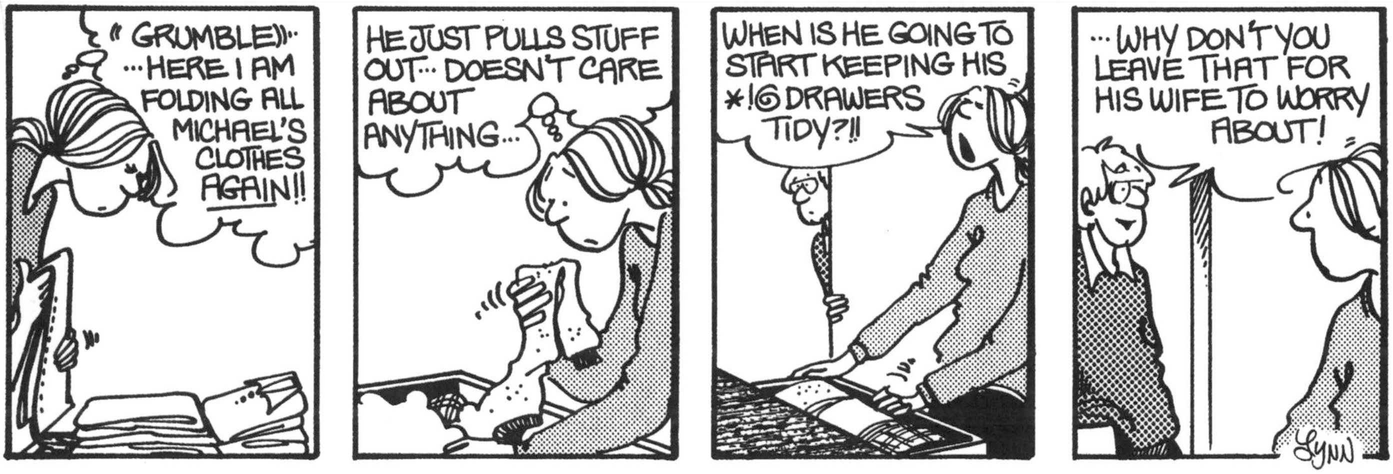
"GRUMBLE"... HERE I AM FOLDING ALL MICHAEL'S CLOTHES AGAIN!!
HE JUST PULLS STUFF OUT... DOESN'T CARE ABOUT ANYTHING...
WHEN IS HE GOING TO START KEEPING HIS *!@ DRAWERS TIDY?!!
...WHY DON'T YOU LEAVE THAT FOR HIS WIFE TO WORRY ABOUT!
LYNN

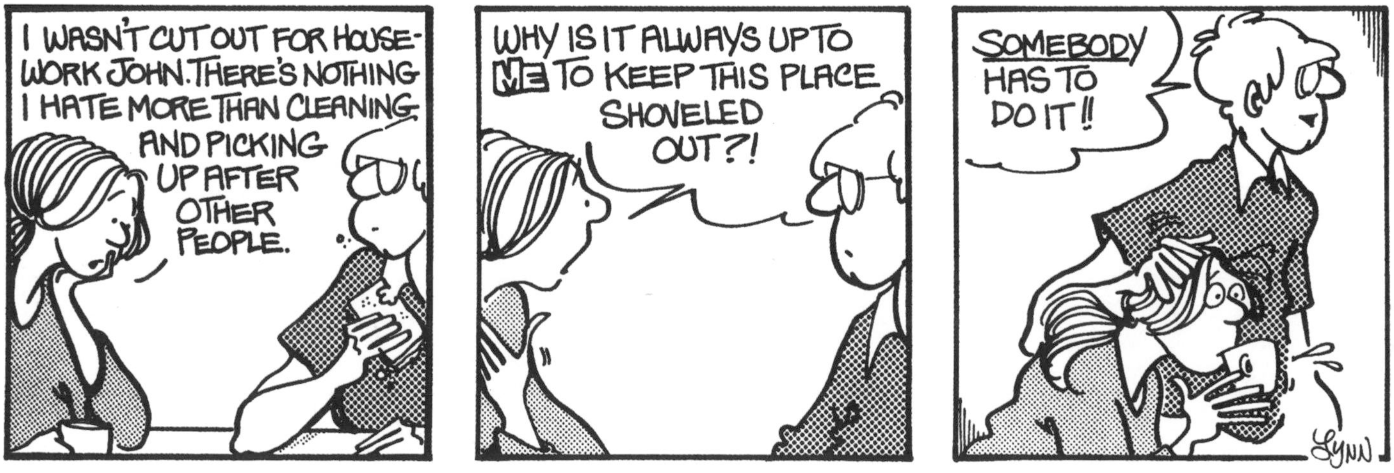
I WASN'T CUT OUT FOR HOUSE-WORK JOHN. THERE'S NOTHING I HATE MORE THAN CLEANING AND PICKING UP AFTER OTHER PEOPLE.
WHY IS IT ALWAYS UP TO ME TO KEEP THIS PLACE SHOVELED OUT?!
SOMEBODY HAS TO DO IT!!
LYNN

BOY, MOM SURE IS A GROUCH TODAY.... WHAT'S BUGGING HER?

IT'S HORMONES, MIKE. SOMETHING PECULIAR TO WOMEN. MAKES 'EM MOODY FROM TIME TO TIME.

I HEARD THAT! THERE'S NOTHING WRONG WITH ME. I'M JUST SICK OF PICKING UP AFTER *YOU!*

I SEE WHAT YOU MEAN.

YOU'RE RIGHT, JOHN - IT'S HORMONES.

ELLY'S GETTING ON IN YEARS. SHE'S OVER 35. SHE COULD BE HEADING INTO THE "CHANGE OF LIFE."

HAVE YOU NOTICED ANY RADICAL MOOD SWINGS?

YEAH...

BUT IT'S MORE LIKE A STRONG LEFT HOOK!

THERE'S NOTHING WRONG WITH ME, JOHN! IT'S JUST HARD FOR ME TO BE NEEDED IN TWO PLACES AT ONCE!

I GO TO WORK - AND WORK LIKE CRAZY - THEN I COME HOME AND WORK LIKE CRAZY. IT'S STARTING TO GET ME DOWN!

IF IT'S TOO MUCH FOR YOU, ELLY..... WHY DON'T YOU QUIT THE JOB?

WHICH ONE?

I have always needed a career. I needed to express myself creatively. I needed to earn my own living, and I needed the companionship of other adults. Even though I felt guilty for putting Aaron in daycare, I was a better parent because I was working. I was also able to pay the bills! The alternative at the time was to go on welfare, and I wanted so badly to avoid this.

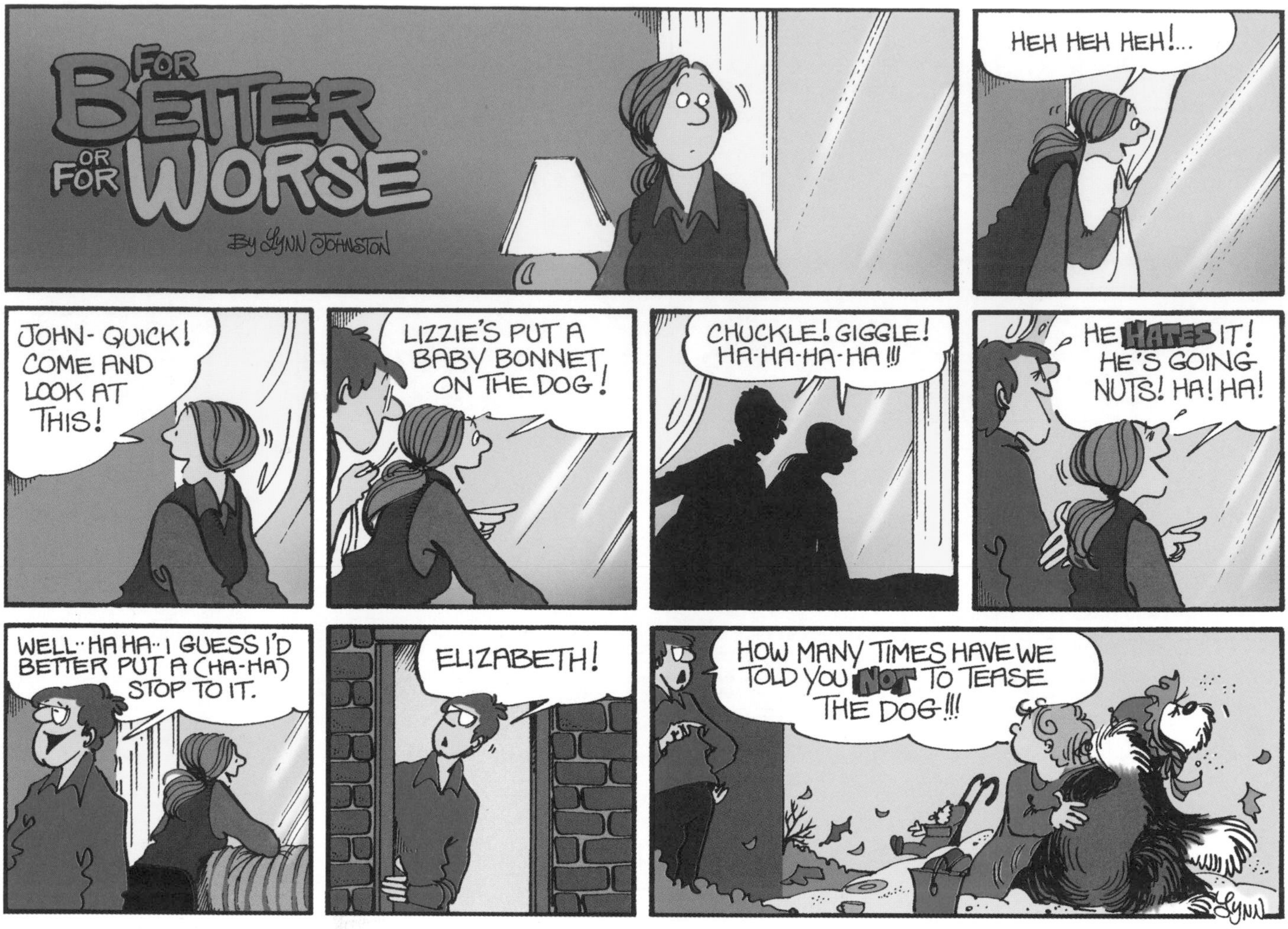
For Better or For Worse
By Lynn Johnston
HEH HEH HEH!...
JOHN- QUICK! COME AND LOOK AT THIS!
LIZZIE'S PUT A BABY BONNET ON THE DOG!
CHUCKLE! GIGGLE! HA-HA-HA-HA!!!
HE HATES IT! HE'S GOING NUTS! HA! HA!
WELL.. HA HA.. I GUESS I'D BETTER PUT A (HA-HA) STOP TO IT.
ELIZABETH!
HOW MANY TIMES HAVE WE TOLD YOU NOT TO TEASE THE DOG!!!
LYNN

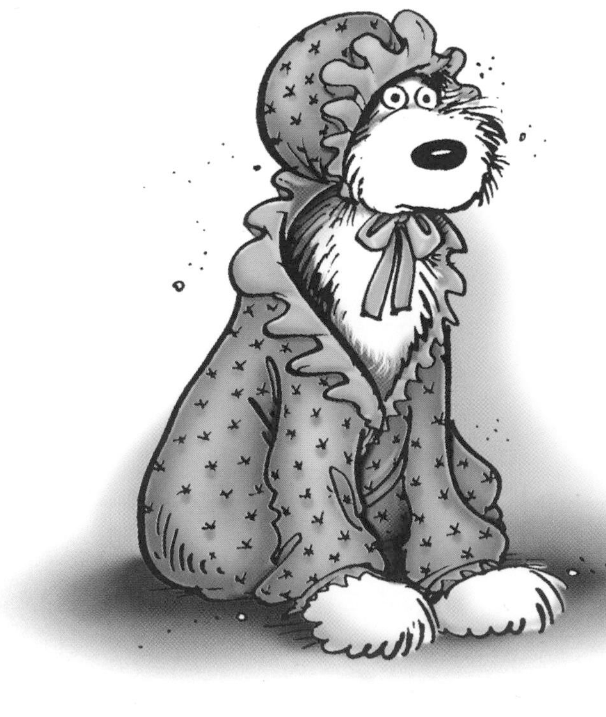

As a kid, I had a talent for making insults. This "gift" could be quite a threat. Woe to the child who had a name that rhymed with something funny or initials that spelled a word. If I was suffering at the hands of a bully, I'd go into my repertoire of insults and "win." When I began to change from kid to teenager, however, I became a butterball, and if somebody called me "fatso," I'd crumble. What goes 'round, comes 'round!

My brother and I fought like crazy until we were both safely out of the house and on our own. Now, in our sixties, we are the best of friends. We've talked about our childhood and tried to figure out why we were so hard on each other. There are many reasons. I guess the old Smothers Brothers line "Mom always liked you best" was part of it. We were also creative, competitive, and bored. Yes, it's a family fact: Boredom is nicely relieved by a good dust-up!

Like Michael, I wanted my room to remain in a constant state of upheaval when I was a kid. The mess was a sign of independence, a statement that marked my room as mine. Commands to clean it up were greeted with indifference. Even if I was forced to comply, the state of "tidy" might have only lasted a day. I could never see the reason why a room had to be kept in order if nobody saw it but me. A kid needs solid reasons, and the threat of punishment wasn't reason enough!

...NOW...I PUT THE KNIFE AN' FORK INNA GLASS LIKE DIS...

ELIZABETH!! THAT'S NO WAY TO SET A TABLE!

OH. YEAH.

I FORGOT PLATES!

YEAH, MOM. I FINALLY GOT THE KIDS TO START PITCHING IN AROUND HERE AND PICK UP AFTER THEM-SELVES!

OH, IT TOOK SOME TIME. I HAD TO FIGHT ...I HAD TO THREATEN -BUT I DID IT!

RIGHT...UH HUH...OVER ONE HURDLE AND ONTO THE NEXT.

SO... WE'VE MADE A DEAL. HE HELPS OUT WITH THE HOUSEWORK ON THE DAYS I WORK...

...AND I TAKE CARE OF IT ON THE DAYS I'M HOME.

SOUNDS GOOD TO ME!

WHAT KIND OF FEMINIST LOGIC DID YOU USE ON HIM THIS TIME?

I CRIED.

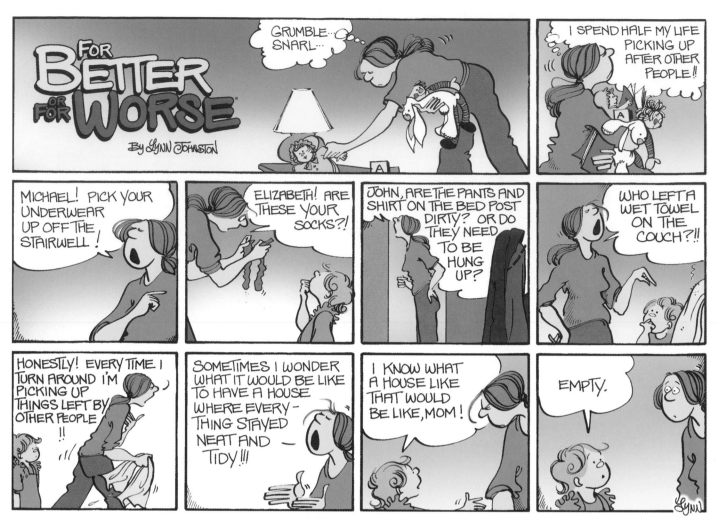

For years, I looked around my busy house wishing things would stay in place, wishing there were no towels on the floor, no sand in the hallway, no toys on the stairs. Then my kids grew up and left home. For years, I had a perfectly tidy house. My dear friend Janet helped me to keep it immaculate. My kitchen sparkled, and my collection of knick-knacks stayed dust free. I truly enjoyed my organized and consistent environment.

Eventually, however, Elizabeth's comment in this Sunday strip came true. My home was neat but empty. It was missing something. Then, my beautiful little granddaughter was born. I have a bouncer and a bassinette in my living room now. Infant toys are piled behind my reading chair, and I'll soon be putting away anything that can be knocked down and broken. I'll have to secure the cupboard doors where breakable things are kept or store them elsewhere. With a toddler around, my house is going to become chaos once more — and I'm looking forward to it. I know how fast she will grow, how soon she'll be gone, and how much I'll miss her.

Allowing Aaron to stay home while I went shopping was a privilege for both of us. He was a responsible kid, and his grandparents lived next door. As far as I know, he didn't get into any mischief, but I was always on my guard. All I had to do was remember what my brother and I did when given the run of the house.

For years Mom and Dad worked in our small jewellery shop on upper Lonsdale in North Vancouver. It took twenty minutes for them to walk home, so we could gauge almost to the minute when the front door handle would turn. It was my job to get dinner on and Al's job to stay out of my way. Sometimes, dinner was a snap, and I'd take off on my bike until the folks arrived. During these times of freedom, Al (aged 13 or 14 at the time) emptied Dad's gin, substituting the missing booze with water. He ate whatever candy was hidden and smoked Dad's cigarettes. I thought he'd be in for it, but he never got caught.

I explored every drawer and every crevice in our house looking for treasure or secrets or hidden birthday gifts. I tried on my mother's underwear and used her perfume. I made crank phone calls and listened in to the party line. (This was a forbidden indiscretion, but I saw Mom do it as well.) I ate stuff and danced on the sofa and felt the freedom I longed for. Freedom then was having the house to myself.

It was with these memories in mind that I looked for evidence of similar lawlessness when Aaron was left alone. I never saw a thing. Obviously, he was as good at covering his tracks as we were!

During my coffee house days, I was often among the great and wanna-be greats of the folk music scene. One evening I joined a group of musician friends for beer and pizza. The young man sitting next to me was rapping constantly on the table, ignoring our pained expressions. Fed up, I put my hand over his the way a mother would silence a child. He was furious! Turned out he was the drummer for a famous group. He did stop tapping, however, for which everyone was grateful!

Alan's adjustment from singlehood to his relationship with Joan was a constant source of comedy. The thing I love about my brother is the way he greets adversity; he makes it into a story, which he embellishes just enough to make it great.

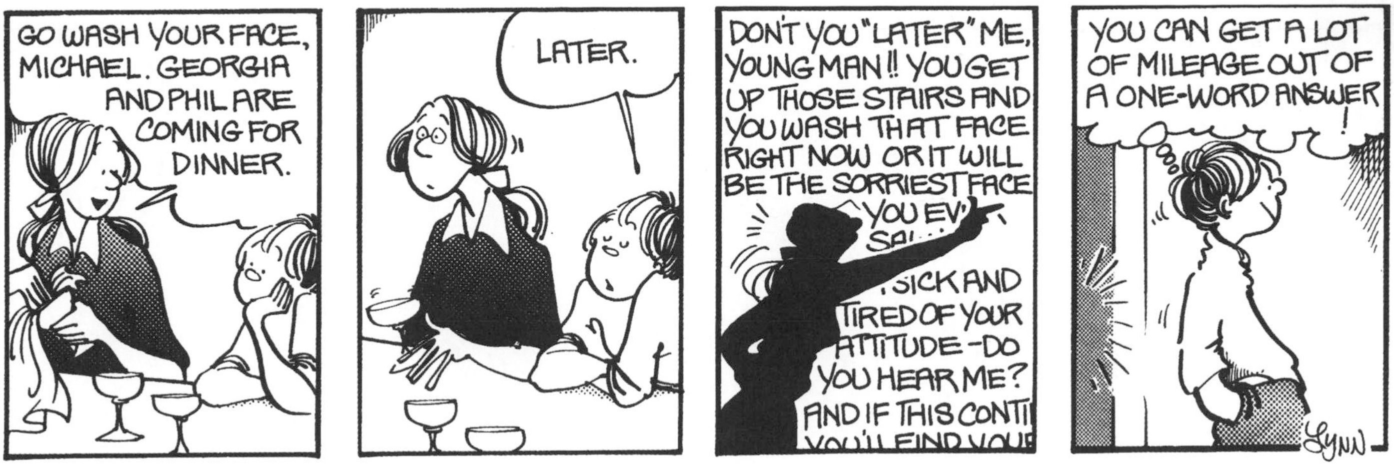
GO WASH YOUR FACE, MICHAEL. GEORGIA AND PHIL ARE COMING FOR DINNER.
LATER.
DON'T YOU "LATER" ME, YOUNG MAN!! YOU GET UP THOSE STAIRS AND YOU WASH THAT FACE RIGHT NOW OR IT WILL BE THE SORRIEST FACE YOU EV
SICK AND TIRED OF YOUR ATTITUDE -DO YOU HEAR ME? AND IF THIS CONTI
YOU CAN GET A LOT OF MILEAGE OUT OF A ONE-WORD ANSWER!
LYNN

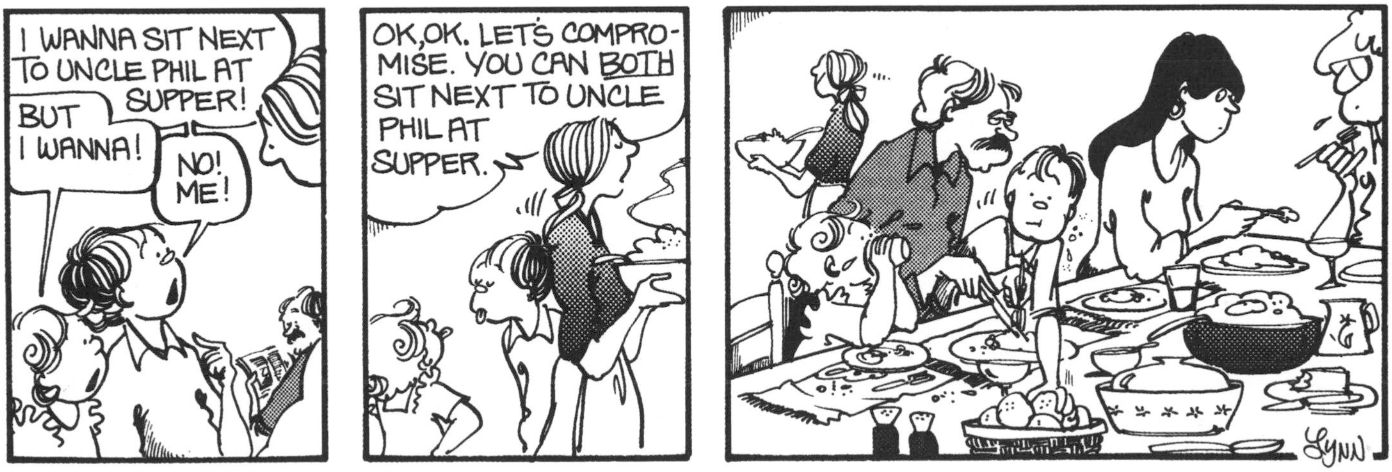
I WANNA SIT NEXT TO UNCLE PHIL AT SUPPER!
BUT I WANNA!
NO! ME!
OK, OK. LET'S COMPROMISE. YOU CAN BOTH SIT NEXT TO UNCLE PHIL AT SUPPER.
LYNN

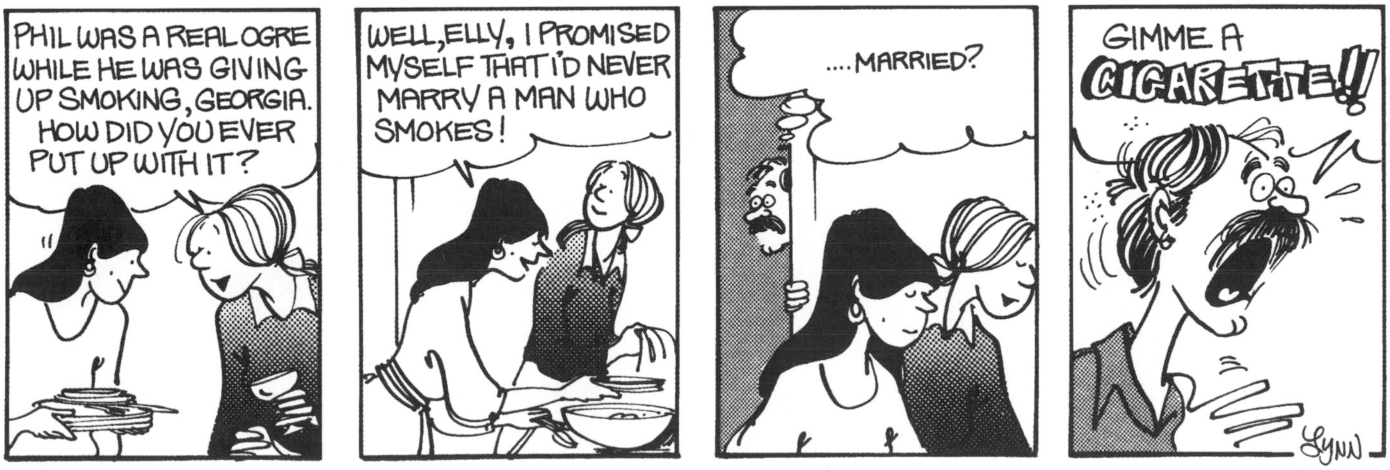
PHIL WAS A REAL OGRE WHILE HE WAS GIVING UP SMOKING, GEORGIA. HOW DID YOU EVER PUT UP WITH IT?
WELL, ELLY, I PROMISED MYSELF THAT I'D NEVER MARRY A MAN WHO SMOKES!
....MARRIED?
GIMME A CIGARETTE!!
LYNN

My mother joined a weight loss program for which she needed one of those tiny food scales. After buying both Alan and me a pack of Smarties, she actually weighed them to prove that neither of us was getting more than the other.

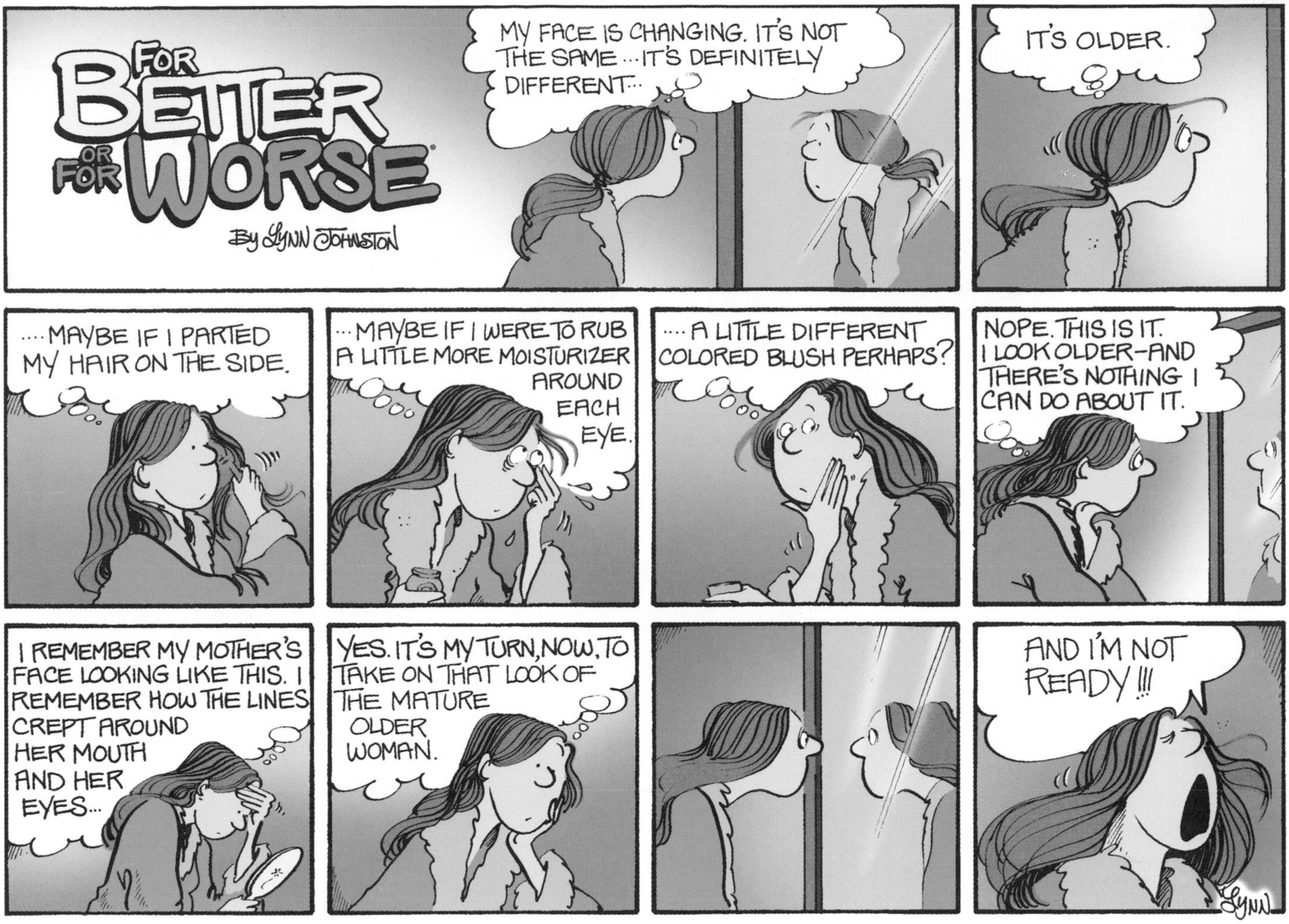
FOR BETTER OR FOR WORSE
BY LYNN JOHNSTON
MY FACE IS CHANGING. IT'S NOT THE SAME ... IT'S DEFINITELY DIFFERENT...
IT'S OLDER.
.... MAYBE IF I PARTED MY HAIR ON THE SIDE.
... MAYBE IF I WERE TO RUB A LITTLE MORE MOISTURIZER AROUND EACH EYE.
.... A LITTLE DIFFERENT COLORED BLUSH PERHAPS?
NOPE. THIS IS IT. I LOOK OLDER-AND THERE'S NOTHING I CAN DO ABOUT IT.
I REMEMBER MY MOTHER'S FACE LOOKING LIKE THIS. I REMEMBER HOW THE LINES CREPT AROUND HER MOUTH AND HER EYES...
YES. IT'S MY TURN, NOW, TO TAKE ON THAT LOOK OF THE MATURE OLDER WOMAN.
AND I'M NOT READY!!!
LYNN

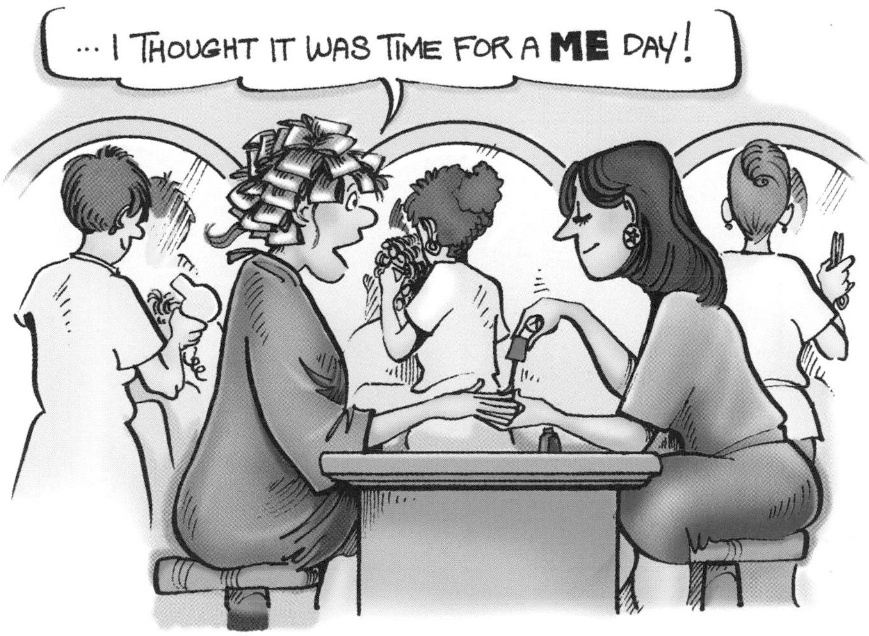
... I THOUGHT IT WAS TIME FOR A **ME** DAY!

When I was growing up, there were a lot of stay-at-home moms. Ours was the one who bandaged knees, handed out cookies, made the bathroom available, and let us play in the sprinkler. So many times we had all the kids over, so many times the parties were at our house, and I remember my exhausted mom saying, "Why is it always my house? Why can't someone ELSE have them over?" When the other moms explained that they were busy, she almost cried — she was busier than anyone!

Aaron and some of his Lynn Lake buddies.

Because Aaron was four years older than Katie, she was left out of a lot of activities. She couldn't race away on her bike or cross the street alone or camp out with the boys in the backyard. She became attached to her dad (since I was working full time in the house) and spent hours with him in his workshop learning how to glue things and make stuff. I think this is why she is so comfortable with tools and to this day can build or fix just about anything!

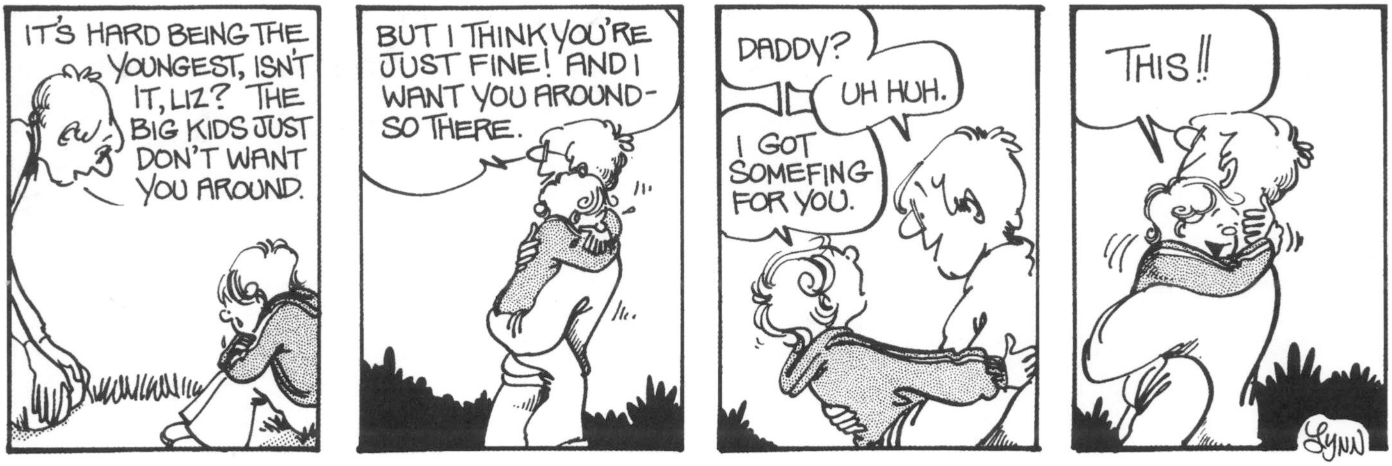
IT'S HARD BEING THE YOUNGEST, ISN'T IT, LIZ? THE BIG KIDS JUST DON'T WANT YOU AROUND.
BUT I THINK YOU'RE JUST FINE! AND I WANT YOU AROUND - SO THERE.
DADDY?
UH HUH.
I GOT SOMEFING FOR YOU.
THIS!!
LYNN

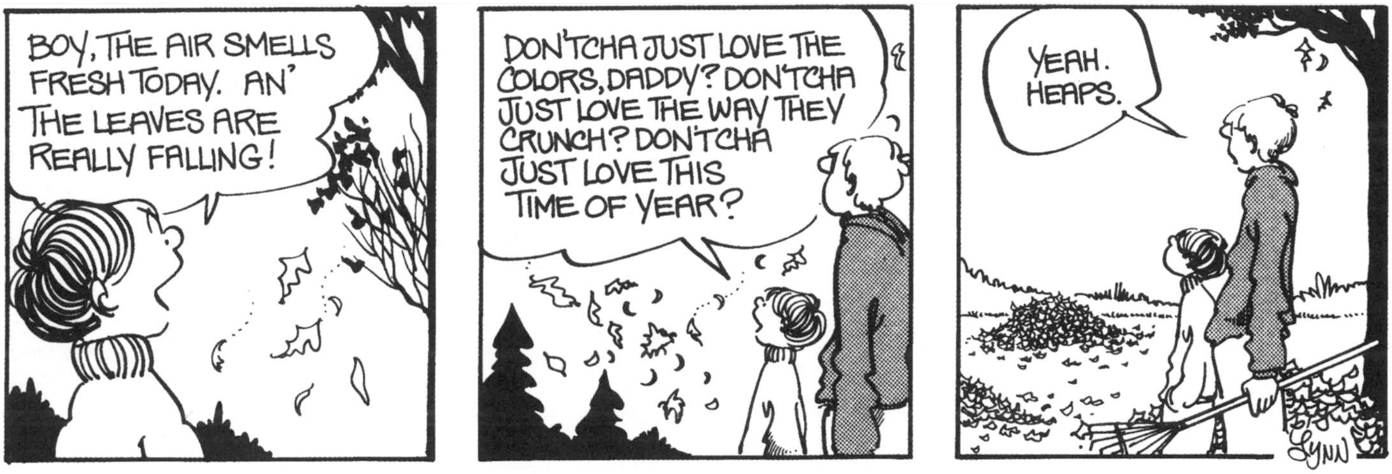
BOY, THE AIR SMELLS FRESH TODAY. AN' THE LEAVES ARE REALLY FALLING!
DON'TCHA JUST LOVE THE COLORS, DADDY? DON'TCHA JUST LOVE THE WAY THEY CRUNCH? DON'TCHA JUST LOVE THIS TIME OF YEAR?
YEAH. HEAPS.
LYNN

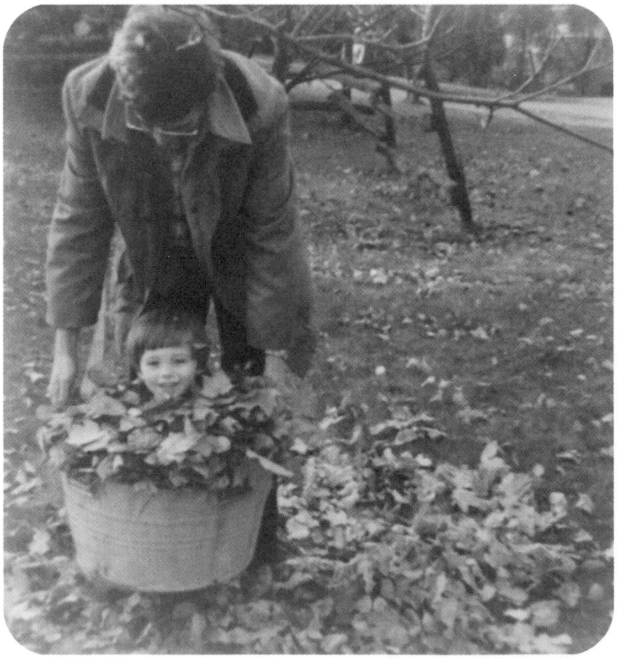

One of the children's books I loved best was about a family of rabbits who painted the woods with all the colours of the rainbow. In spring they painted the buds bright green, in the fall they painted the leaves different colours, and in winter, they painted the shadows on the snow. Even now, whenever I see long turquoise-grey shadows stretching across a snowy lane, I remember the illustrations in that book.

MOM, I GOT LIZZIE ALL DRESSED UP FOR HALLOWEEN, AN' YOU GOTTA GUESS WHAT SHE IS!

HMM. IS SHE A CLOWN? NOPE.. LITTLE RED RIDING HOOD? NOPE.. A LITTLE GHOSTIE? NOPE. A BALLERINA? NOPE..

OK, I GIVE UP. WHAT IS SHE?

A PUNK ROCKER!!

AW, COME ON, MOM — SHE WANTS TO BE A PUNK ROCKER FOR HALLOWEEN, DON'T YOU, LIZ!

HEY, SHOW MOM SOME MEAN FACES! YEAH — NOW ACT ALL COOL LIKE!

MICHAEL, THAT LOOKS ABSOLUTELY AWFUL! IT DOES?

KID, YOU'RE DOING GREAT!

ELIZABETH — A PUNK ROCKER, OF ALL THINGS!

ALL THE KIDS LIKE TO DRESS UP AS VIDEO STARS, EL! IT'S ONLY A COSTUME!

HECK, IT DOESN'T PHASE ME ONE BIT!

GOOD. MICHAEL WANTS TO BE BOY GEORGE.

WOW, MAN! LOOKIT THIS! THEY'RE GONNA BE SHOWIN' SCARY FLICKS ON CHANNEL 5 ALL NEXT WEEK!

WOULDN'T IT BE NEAT IF "GREMLINS" WAS ON?

YEAH! GROSS! 'MEMBER THE GUY BLOWS UP IN THE MICROWAVE? YEAH! EVER SICK! YOU SAW GUTS AN' EVERYTHING!

SIGH... WHAT EVER HAPPENED TO "THE SOUND OF MUSIC"?

MOM? MOM! CAN YOU HELP ME, PLEASE? MOM? MOMMY! MOM, I CAN'T DO THIS - YOU DO IT! CUT IT FOR ME! HELP ME, MOM! MOMMY! MOM! MOM?

THERE!!

BOY! ISN'T IT A GOOD THING DAD SAID WE COULD EACH DO OUR OWN PUMPKIN!!

177

Like me, Aaron and Katie truly appreciate good costumes. Every year at Halloween, they just had to look in the costume box or make a suggestion, and we had a plan. We would all get into the spirit of making wearable art. There was nothing too complicated or too farfetched for us to make, and, like Alan and me, our kids had the best homemade outfits ever (if I do say so myself). We had a Sherlock Holmes hat, pipe, and cape, but the year this strip was done, Aaron didn't want to dress as Sherlock. I was insistent and said that all I had to do was make the jacket, but no deal. Instead, he painted himself green and went out as the Hulk. Left to mourn for Holmes, I did this series of strips in his honour.

For years we gave out a Halloween themed dental kit — with brush, paste, and floss included. One time, thinking the kids would be tired of getting toothbrushes, I decided to give out candy like everyone else. The next day, I got calls from a couple of parents asking what had happened to the toothbrushes! Apparently, they counted on Halloween, when every year their kids would get a new one.

The thought of not allowing my kids to dress like punk rockers makes me smile. Unlike some other moms, I encouraged my kids to dye their hair and wear crazy outfits. They wouldn't go for it. Perhaps it's because I insisted, or maybe they weren't into that kind of stuff. Either way, they never did the punk thing, and I'm OK with that, too!

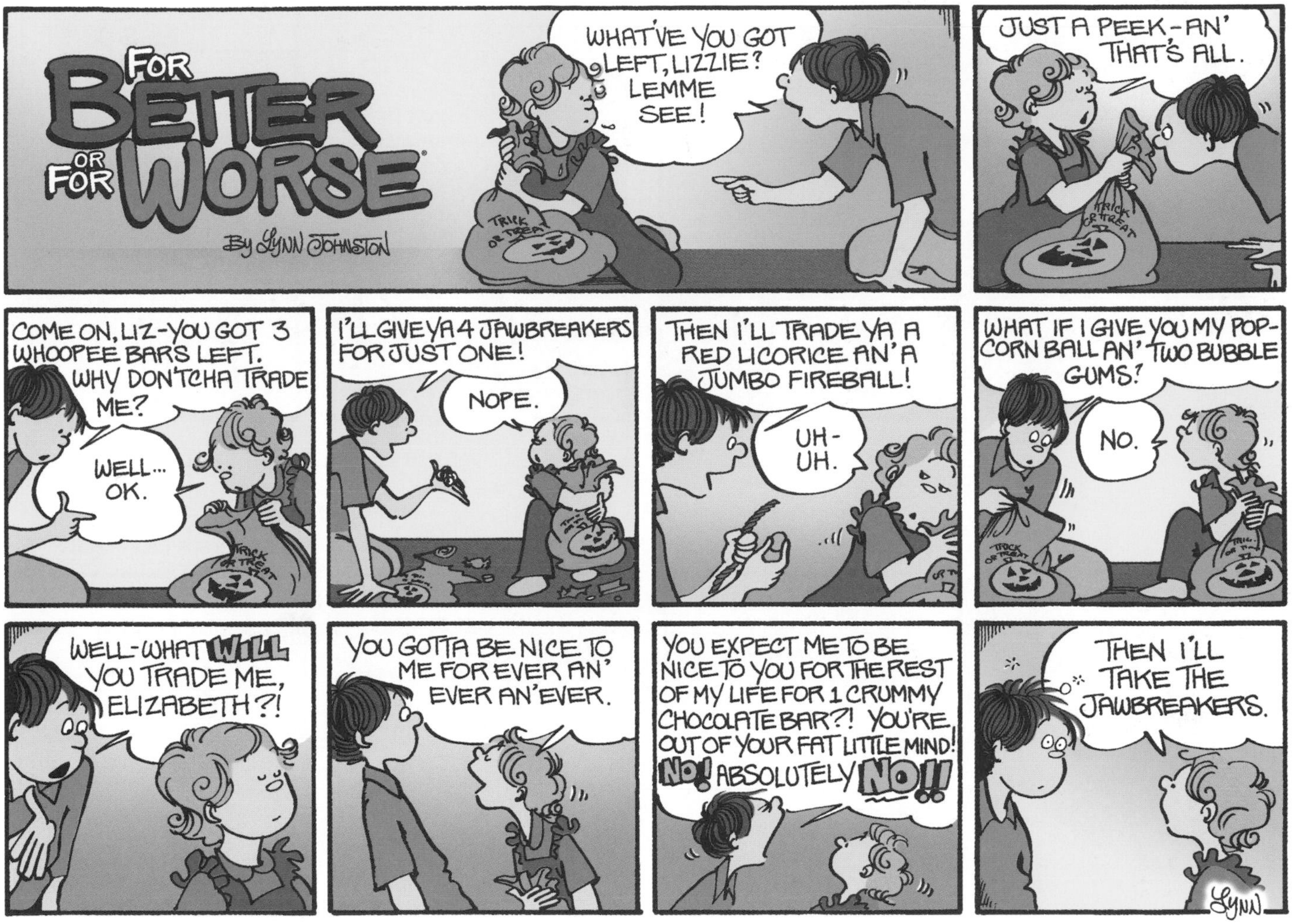
FOR BETTER OR FOR WORSE
BY LYNN JOHNSTON
WHAT'VE YOU GOT LEFT, LIZZIE? LEMME SEE!
TRICK OR TREAT
JUST A PEEK-AN' THAT'S ALL.
COME ON, LIZ-YOU GOT 3 WHOOPEE BARS LEFT.
WHY DON'TCHA TRADE ME?
WELL... OK.
I'LL GIVE YA 4 JAWBREAKERS FOR JUST ONE!
NOPE.
THEN I'LL TRADE YA A RED LICORICE AN' A JUMBO FIREBALL!
UH-UH.
WHAT IF I GIVE YOU MY POP-CORN BALL AN' TWO BUBBLE GUMS?
NO.
WELL-WHAT WILL YOU TRADE ME, ELIZABETH?!
YOU GOTTA BE NICE TO ME FOR EVER AN' EVER AN' EVER.
YOU EXPECT ME TO BE NICE TO YOU FOR THE REST OF MY LIFE FOR 1 CRUMMY CHOCOLATE BAR?! YOU'RE OUT OF YOUR FAT LITTLE MIND! NO! ABSOLUTELY NO!!
THEN I'LL TAKE THE JAWBREAKERS.
LYNN

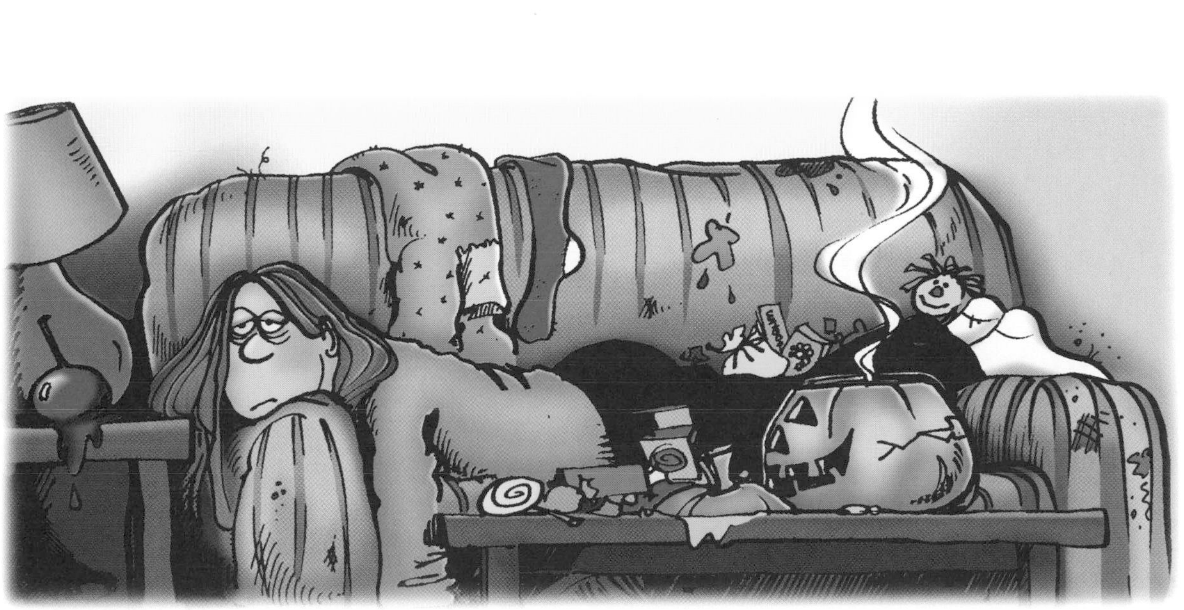

Because I didn't want to juggle a whole team of characters in the dental office, I made Jean both the receptionist and dental assistant. This is impossible! I then added the situation many companies dread: maternity leave.

I don't think I had talked about Jean's private life. Whether she was married or not had never come up, and so this pregnancy was something readers just had to accept. I was still learning how to create a believable and consistent storyline.

For a while, in Rod's clinic, both patient and assistant wore protective garb when x-rays were taken. It was soon evident that the on–off switch could be placed outside the operatory behind a permanent protective shield. This made things much easier.

This storyline was really about the hiring of a new receptionist for the clinic. Our ad in the paper resulted in over a hundred applications. Many of these were instantly set aside due to the reasons I put in this strip!

WHAT'S THE MATTER, MIKE?

THE WHOLE CLASS HAD TO STAY IN AFTER SCHOOL, THAT'S ALL!

AN' WE WEREN'T EVEN DOING ANYTHING! IT'S NO FAIR! A WHOLE CLASS GETS PUNISHED FOR NO REASON!

WE WEREN'T DOING A THING! ... ONE BURP AN' ONE SPITBALL AN' THE WHOLE CLASS ....

I KNEW THERE WAS ANOTHER SIDE TO THE STORY.

WHAT'S FOR SUPPER, MOM?

"WAIT-AND-SEE PUDDING"!

THAT'S WHAT MY GRANDMA WOULD SAY WHENEVER WE ASKED HER THAT QUESTION!

DID MOM SAY WHAT WE'RE HAVIN' FOR SUPPER?

YEAH.

LEFTOVERS.

YOU GONNA HIRE SOMEBODY REAL PRETTY TO BE YOUR NEW ASSISTANT, DADDY?

MICHAEL, DECISIONS LIKE THAT AREN'T BASED ON LOOKS! WE INTERVIEW EVERYONE SERIOUSLY.

MY STAFF AND I HAVE TO CONSIDER THEIR QUALIFICATIONS, EXPERIENCE, ATTITUDE, ABILITY AND REFERENCES ....

... THEN WE HIRE THE ONE YOUR MOTHER LIKES.

After the applications for a new receptionist had been whittled down to a few, we called each girl out of the blue to see what her telephone attitude was like. An answer like, "Who? Who's calling? Hey, you kids shut the H*** up, I'm on the %#*&@^ phone!" was a definite "no."

184

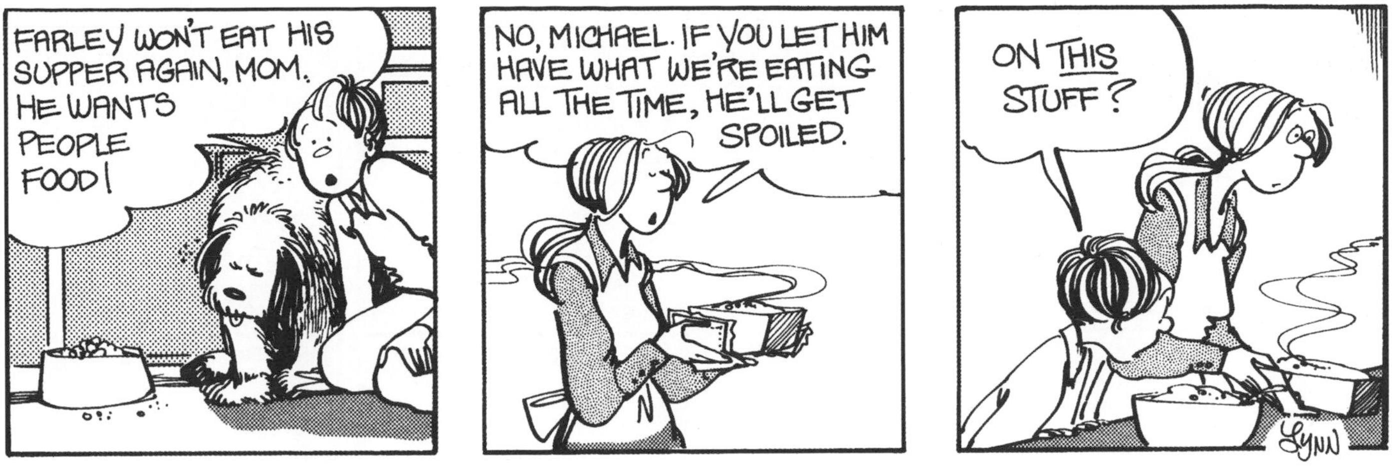
FARLEY WON'T EAT HIS SUPPER AGAIN, MOM. HE WANTS PEOPLE FOOD!
NO, MICHAEL. IF YOU LET HIM HAVE WHAT WE'RE EATING ALL THE TIME, HE'LL GET SPOILED.
ON THIS STUFF?
LYNN

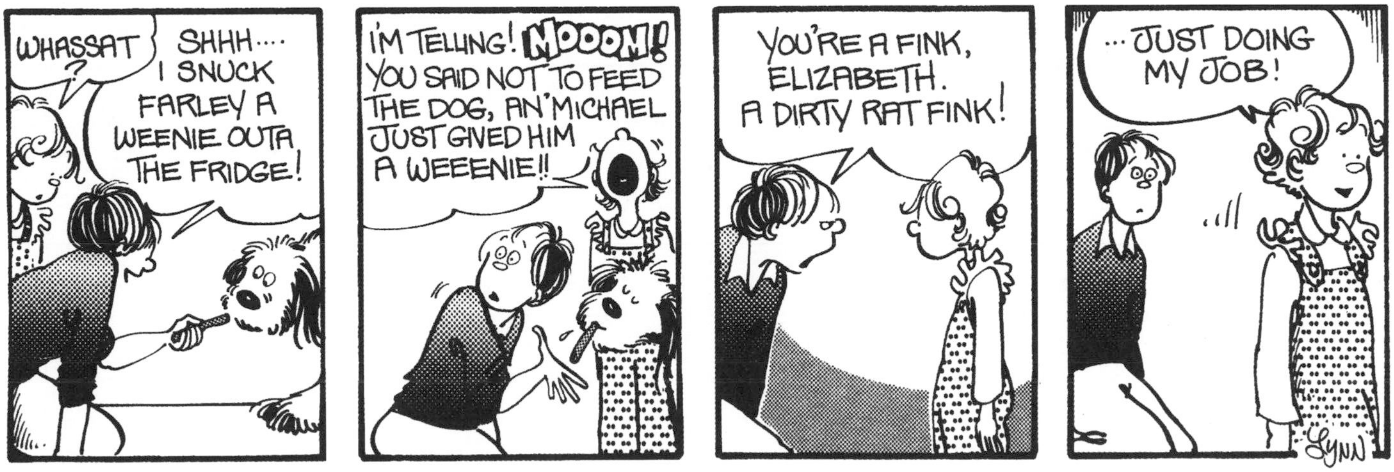
WHASSAT?
SHHH.... I SNUCK FARLEY A WEENIE OUTA THE FRIDGE!
I'M TELLING! MOOOM!
YOU SAID NOT TO FEED THE DOG, AN' MICHAEL JUST GIVED HIM A WEEENIE!!
YOU'RE A FINK, ELIZABETH. A DIRTY RAT FINK!
...JUST DOING MY JOB!
LYNN

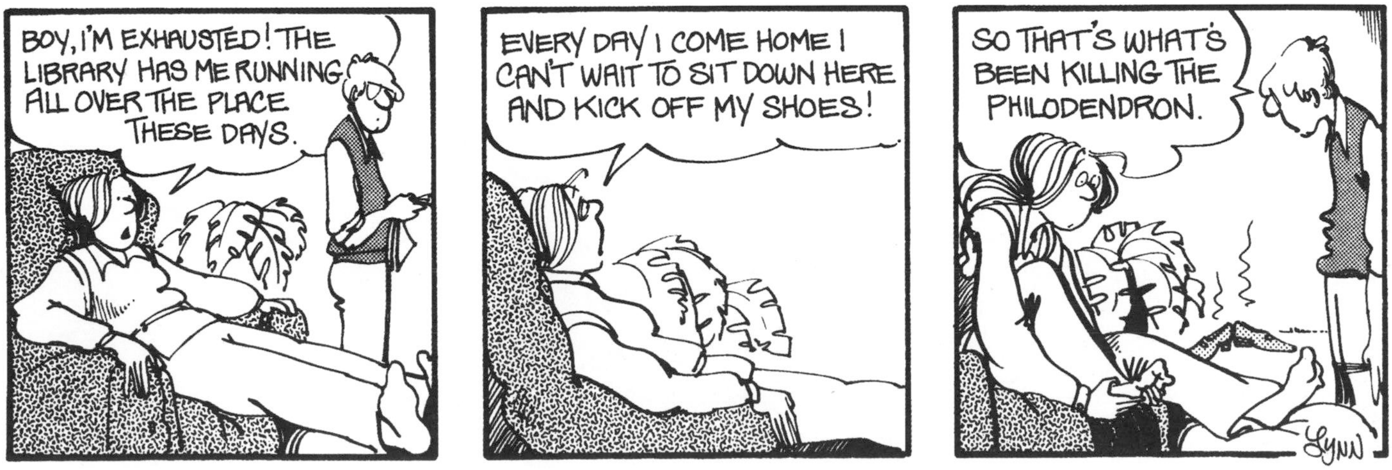
BOY, I'M EXHAUSTED! THE LIBRARY HAS ME RUNNING ALL OVER THE PLACE THESE DAYS.
EVERY DAY I COME HOME I CAN'T WAIT TO SIT DOWN HERE AND KICK OFF MY SHOES!
SO THAT'S WHAT'S BEEN KILLING THE PHILODENDRON.
LYNN

Again, a Sunday strip that didn't have to be invented. Word for word, this was real dialogue, and I wrote it down on a paper towel in the kitchen. I never seemed to have a notebook available. There was one in my bedside table for ideas that came in the night, but during the day, I had to grab whatever scrap of paper I could find. I learned quickly to capture an idea as soon as I could. My chequebook, which was always in my purse (before credit cards), was filled with punch lines, fast sketches, and ideas for future strips. Trying to remember these things later was impossible, and if I let a good one get away, I'd be miserable! This exchange made for a cathartic cartoon and saved my son, once again, from the wrath of Mom.

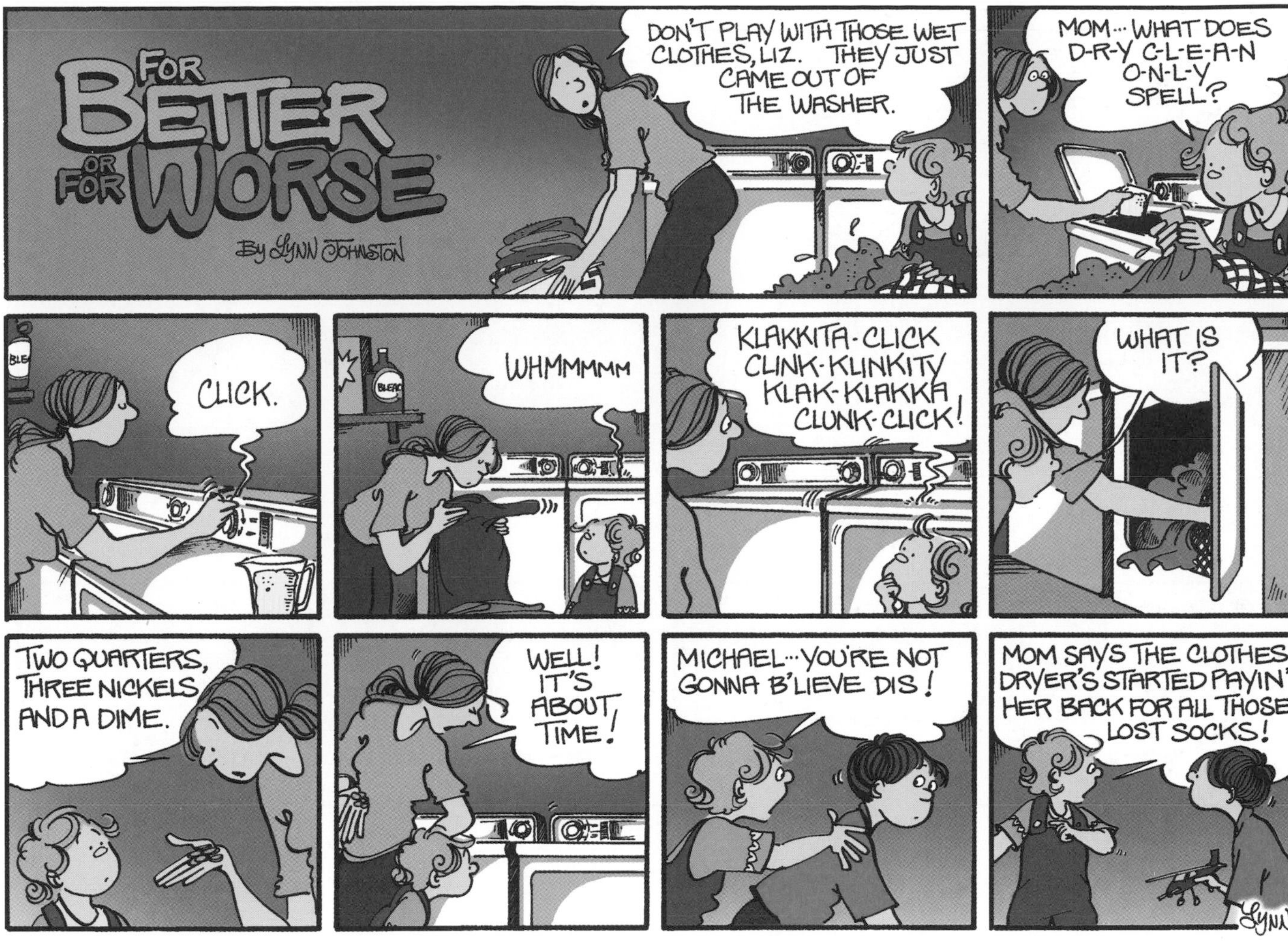
For Better or For Worse
By Lynn Johnston
DON'T PLAY WITH THOSE WET CLOTHES, LIZ. THEY JUST CAME OUT OF THE WASHER.
MOM... WHAT DOES D-R-Y C-L-E-A-N O-N-L-Y SPELL?
CLICK.
WHMMMMM
KLAKKITA-CLICK CLINK-KLINKITY KLAK-KLAKKA CLUNK-CLICK!
WHAT IS IT?
TWO QUARTERS, THREE NICKELS AND A DIME.
WELL! IT'S ABOUT TIME!
MICHAEL... YOU'RE NOT GONNA B'LIEVE DIS!
MOM SAYS THE CLOTHES DRYER'S STARTED PAYIN' HER BACK FOR ALL THOSE LOST SOCKS!
LYNN

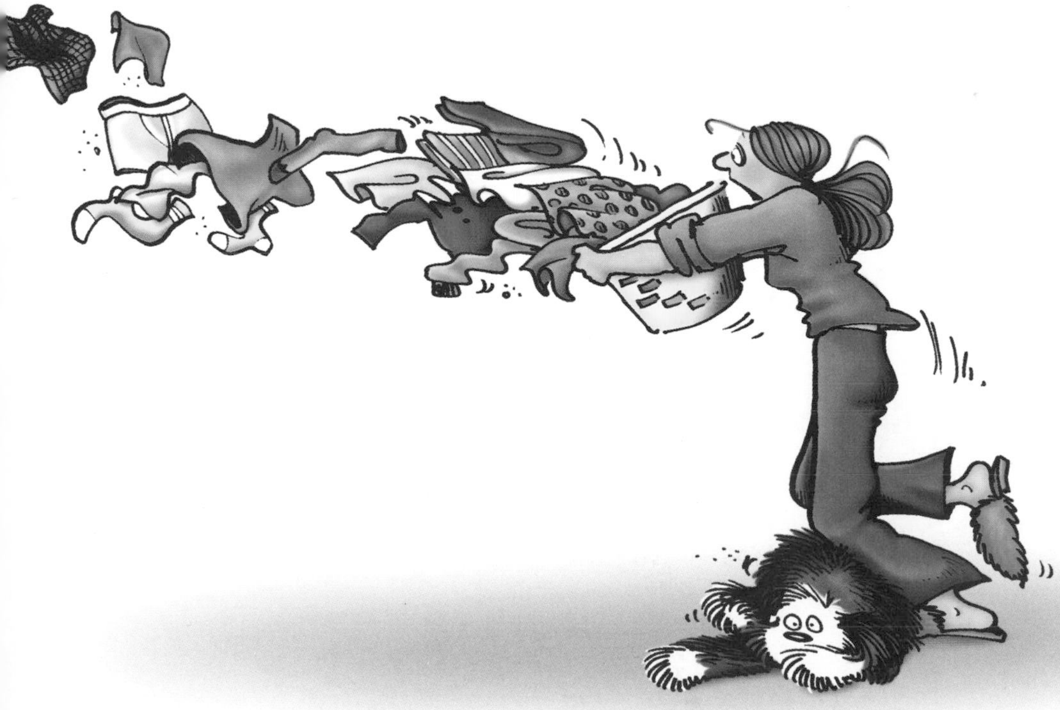

Boys really can smell terrible. A girls' locker room might have its ambient whiff, but a room full of young male hockey players can be downright asphyxiating. When it was decided that moms were no longer required for skate tie-ups and supportive hugs, women rejoiced all over town. The news made rink-side hot dogs and all-day coffee taste fine. It was, let me put it this way, "A breath of fresh air!"

LOOK, MOM! DADDY AN' I MADE A CAKE!

DADDY PUT THE STUFF INNA BOWL, AN' MIXED IT UP, AN' PUT IT INNA PAN AN' DEN INNA OVEN!

I THOUGHT YOU SAID YOU BOTH MADE THE CAKE, LIZZIE. WHAT DID YOU DO?

I HAD TO SHOW HIM WHERE EVERYTHING WAS!

WHAT— YOU'RE NOT FINISHED YET?!!

YOU HAVEN'T GOT YOUR 'JAMAS ON, YOU HAVEN'T DRIED YOUR HAIR... YOU HAVEN'T DONE YOUR TEETH...

WHAT DO I HAVE TO DO — COME UP HERE AND STAND OVER YOU?!

DUMB QUESTION.

WHY DO I HAFTA GO TO BED NOW? I GOT 10 MINUTES LEFT!

BECAUSE THIS IS THE FIRST TIME ALL WEEK THAT YOUR DAD AND I HAVE HAD A CHANCE TO SEE EACH OTHER.

I WANT US TO BE ALONE TOGETHER, LIKE AN OLD HAPPILY MARRIED COUPLE.

GZZNNNNN ZZZMMM

There were times when I envied my dog: no bills to pay, no groceries to buy, just hang around and be loved. On the other hand, boredom and the lack of freedom must drag a guy down.

The other day I watched a young mother guiding her son around the grocery store. She was letting him do all the shopping. She asked him what ingredients he would buy if he was going to make chili and what would make a nice salad. The child was about four years old and right into the project. This was a shopping trip just for him. He had to think about what he was buying and why. He was told about the cost, how one kind of bathroom tissue might be a better value for the family than another. He made decisions about desserts and treats and whether one kind of bread would be more nutritious than another. I was so impressed with this young woman's insight, patience, and ingenuity that I had to compliment her. She just said, "He was interested, so I thought it was time." As I watched her continue to the checkout counter, I wished I'd had her good sense when I was shepherding my little ones!

For this punch line, I wanted to do a gag that was gas-related, but I knew that it wouldn't pass the censors.

After this scenario occurred, the quote "Sorry, I didn't mean to be honest" became one of the many inside jokes we shared.

Yes, this happened, but the toothbrush Aaron used was mine.

For the longest time, the Sears catalogue was our window into the world of new toys. Every Christmas, the special edition came out and was devoured upon delivery. These days the big box stores have it all right there, and the Internet will find you anything "unique." The catalogues are smaller now and feature clothing, mostly. Parents can pick and purchase toys before the book even comes out. Another tradition bows to instant availability!

Putting up Christmas lights on our log house was a challenge. The high peaked roof was a difficult place to climb, and the sides were hard to reach because of a glass porch we'd installed. When we learned that some folks were putting up smaller lights and leaving them all year 'round, we did the same. Still, the image of Dad having to struggle with Christmas lights every year was too good to abandon in the strip!

I'M GOING DOWNTOWN, EL. WANT ANYTHING?

NO, NOT REALLY. BUT JUST A MINUTE.

HERE'S MY SHOPPING LIST. THERE'S STUFF AT THE CLEANERS, GET A BIG TURKEY... AND LIZZIE WANTS TO COME ALONG.

DID SHE START OUT BY SAYING "NOT REALLY"?

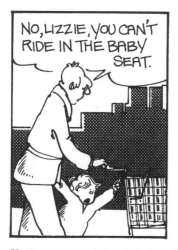

NO, LIZZIE, YOU CAN'T RIDE IN THE BABY SEAT.

YOU'RE TOO BIG! I SAID YOU'RE TOO BIG!

NO. I SAID NO, YOU CAN'T RIDE IN THE BABY SEAT. YOU'RE TOO BIG!!

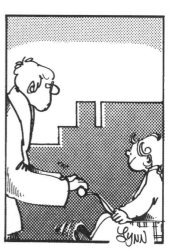

Katie was much too big, but she insisted on riding in the shopping cart baby seat. I told her repeatedly that it wasn't a good idea, but I gave in. As soon as she was settled, she was stuck. I told her to be patient, that we'd get her out when I paid for the groceries. She wailed. The man at the meat counter came out from behind the showcase and lifted Kate's upper half while I pushed her feet. We extracted her without injury. I said nothing. I didn't have to!

YOU TOLD DADDY TO BUY A BIG TURKEY, MOM. HOW BIG A ONE IS HE GONNA GET?

OH, 10-12 LBS. OR SO ... DADDY KNOWS WHAT I MEANT.

HMMM...BIG TURKEY... GET A BIG TURKEY...

CHRISTMAS TURKEYS

25 LBS. SHOULD BE BIG ENOUGH!

This story came about when I picked up a huge turkey by the metal tag and lifted it into my cart. It occurred to me that I had done something really stupid. The turkey weighed at least eighteen pounds, and if I'd dropped it, I could have broken a foot!

The thought of someone struggling with a turkey-induced injury made me laugh, and so I inflicted this on poor John.

I was sure that with the huge number of readers seeing this story, surely there was someone out there who had experienced this very thing. I decided to give one of these original strips to the first person who wrote and told me their story.

Sure enough, a man from Ohio sent a letter telling me that he had indeed broken his foot by lifting a heavy frozen turkey by the tag, breaking the wire tie. The worst part of his injury, he confessed, was that nobody felt sorry for him. He said that as soon as they heard how it happened, they laughed. "If I had been skiing or hiking and had broken my foot, I'd have had some sympathy!" he moaned. I sent him a strip. He wrote back to say it made him feel better!

I had a number of complaints about "violence" in this scenario. These same people said nothing about the cruel injury suffered by our hero in the previous strips!

We always had bubble lights on our tree when Alan and I were young. They were our favourite ornaments. We loved to play with them and take them apart. One Christmas, Alan was very sick. He had a high fever, and just to prove it, he put the glass tube from a bubble light in his mouth — and it bubbled! What a nifty thermometer! We thought Mom would be angry, but she wasn't. When you're feeling miserable on Christmas morning, anything that makes you smile is just fine.

Alan and me wearing Mom's hand-knit
Christmas sweaters.

When I believed in Santa Claus, I thought he, like God, could see me and know what I was thinking wherever I was. When my mother finally told me that Santa was imaginary, I wasn't disappointed … I was relieved! It was a coming of age, I guess, and the exciting part was keeping the magic alive for the kids who were younger than I was.

This was a rare opportunity to use an expletive … without profanity. I liked this one!

THE KIDS ARE ASLEEP ALREADY? THAT'S AMAZING!

YEAH... I REMEMBER WHEN I WAS THEIR AGE LYING AWAKE... TOO EXCITED ABOUT SANTA TO EVEN THINK ABOUT SLEEPING!

ME, TOO. I COULD NEVER SLEEP ON CHRISTMAS EVE WHEN I WAS LITTLE.

HEH, HEH... WELL, G'NIGHT, HONEY.

I CAN'T SLEEP.

...FOR WHAT WE ARE ABOUT TO RECEIVE, MAY THE LORD MAKE US TRULY....

This is the prayer my grandfather always said before a big meal. "For what we are about to receive, may the lord make us truly thankful." We thought it was a great prayer. It was sincere. It was genuinely heartfelt, and it said what needed to be said — before the gravy got cold!

STOMP CLUMP STOMP CLUMP STOMP CLUMP

HI, JOHN! WHAT DID YOU GET FOR CHRISTMAS?

JUST WHAT I WANTED.

SKIS.

Christmas has always been my favourite time of year. I start looking for the perfect gifts in January and continue on until December. Funny stuff is best, and when I find the perfect thing for the perfect person, I can hardly wait to wrap it and give it away. Maybe it's because we had so little when I was young that makes shopping such a treat. My brother and I were lucky to get one special toy. Anything else had to be useful — like clothes or school supplies. We learned to save and to spend judiciously. When birthdays or Christmas came the suspense was awful; knowing we might get something we had been longing for — if we could afford it. Even now I wonder what our parents did without so Alan and I could have something special for Christmas.

Our parents were adept at making ends meet. Even though we had little to live on, we had everything. In looking back, I can see that we had what mattered most: a solid, caring family, a comfortable home, good friends, and confidence in the future. This is what I tried to portray in *For Better or For Worse*. No matter what happened, there was always something good to look forward to ... we are now looking forward to creating treasury number four!